W9-AAU-412

GREENER PASTURES

The Success Book
–Told with Humor

---

by
Roy Pinyoun

Roy Pinyoun
7005 Sandy Forks Rd.
Raleigh, N.C. 27609
Suite C-3

PRINTED IN THE UNITED STATES OF AMERICA BY
EDWARDS & BROUGHTON CO., RALEIGH, NORTH CAROLINA

FOREWORD

Greener Pastures is an easy reading collection of success stories, blended with appropriate humor.

It is a book that could help you find your "greener pastures," whether you are to be more successful, have more wealth, get a promotion, or just live a more rewarding, happy, harmonious life.

Greener Pastures tells about all people, the uneducated, the poor, the handicapped and the aged, who found their greener pastures.

They found their greener pastures by using the same blessings that you have, namely, courage, determination, faith, desire, ambition and a positive mental attitude.

Leonardo da Vinci said, "Oh God what you give for the price of an effort."

It is the programmed effort that is responsible for everything we use, everything we come in contact with and everything we have.

Someone, somewhere, somehow had to be motivated to create this effort for his or her betterment.

Perhaps you, too, will find the stimuli, reading this book, to motivate you to unlock the door to the riches you have untapped within.

Too many people pass opportunity by and wait. They wait for the spring, they wait for the summer, then the fall and winter. They keep waiting and wishing, wanting and wondering, plotting and planning, dreaming and hoping and praying for something to happen. What they don't realize is — they have to make it happen.

It is hoped that *Greener Pastures* will make it happen for you. When it happens, and it will, you will realize it all started from within you. For your world without is a reflection of your world within; and if you are looking anywhere else, you are wasting your time.

DEDICATION

To my son, Jeff

GREENER PASTURES

We sometimes get the feeling,
Pastures are greener up the road.
And sometimes have the feeling
We're carrying the heavier load.

We'd like to be like the other guy,
Who seems to have it good.
But the other guy is watching us,
And he'd change if he could.

Each one is looking quite envious,
At the other one's domain.
And each is wishing his might be
Somehow, just the same.

What we are and what we would be,
The goodness and the sin,
Is in each one of us to find,
It's waiting deep within.

—Roy Pinyoun

CONTENTS

Page

The Candy Stand 1
J. C. Penney, Fish Market, Orchids
Wind the Clock 5
Charlie McCarthy, Irving Berlin, War Bonds
You Can Do It 8
Gillette, Ulysses S. Grant, J. D. Rockefeller
Packy 10
Bob Hope, Mark Twain, Wm. Taft
Hope 14
Coca Cola
The Real Fortune 16
(Poem)
Opportunity 17
Sir Walter Raleigh
The Door Opens 20
(Poem)
The Echo 21
Angry Miners
The Happy Man 22
(Poem)
Perfect 23
As We Think 25
Contractor—Little Old Lady
Socrates 29
Fran Tarkenton
The Auction 31
DuPont, the Maid
Persistence 35
Standard Oil
Goals 37
Conrad Hilton, Thomas Edison
The Tigers 41
Boxers, Jack Dempsey
The King of the Jungle 44
River Boat
Courage 45
Pete Gray, Marie, Walt Disney, Monopoly
Uncle Tom's Cabin, Magician, Suicide
Thinking 50
Archimedes, the Barber, Women
A Piece of Iron 54
Roger Williams, the Other Guy
Open the Door 58
Bernard Baruch
Nothing To Unload 60
Children 61
Halloween, Catholic Lady
What Do You See 63
The Race Horse
Be a Starter 66
J. Paul Getty, Church Meeting, Picture of God
Time 69
African Tribe

Page

The Difference 71
(Poem)
The Piece of Sugar 72
Bernard Baruch, State Fair
The Pelicans 74
Shrimp Boats
Be Prepared 76
Clarence Birdseye, Boy Scouts, Harvey Cushman
Silence 79
George Jessel
Keep Knocking 80
The Gun Company, Johnny Weissmuller
The Volcano 82
Vital 5% 84
Blue Belle
The Day That Passed Away 86
The Breakfast 87
State Fair, Harold Conway, Balloons
Keeping On 89
Carter Ain't Comin' 90
Love 92
Babe Ruth, William Bendix
The Helper 94
The Saw 96
Science Teacher
Counterfeit 98
Henry Ford
Thank You 100
Western Union, Sugardaddy
Fear 103
George Allen
Wish 106
The Busy Man 108
The Gorilla
The Neighborhood 110
Christopher Columbus, Leonardo da Vinci
It's the Decisions 112
Abe Lincoln
You 114
Russians, Merchandise
Dedication 119
Charles Atlas, Walter Chysler, Floor Show
It's Your Time 122
Orville and Wilbur Wright
I'd Been a Janitor 124
Frank Woolworth
The Chandelier 126
They Laughed 128
Enthusiasm 130
Glasses, Dog Food, National Cash Register
Two Bucks 135
Shoe Company
Plainfield State Teachers 137
Count Your Blessings 140

THE CANDY STAND

At the turn of the century a young fellow had a small candy stand on the boardwalk of Atlantic City. One night the sea became so rough that the waves washed in on his supply of candy. With a supply of water-soaked candy on hand he advertised, "Salt water is good for candy." It was the beginning of salt water taffy.

We have seen obstacles turn people into "quitters." Most people would have quit if they had encountered the misfortune of this young fellow and the candy stand. Instead of thinking of all the reasons why he should quit, he asked himself "What can I do?" He did it!

In the book, *Think and Grow Rich,* Napoleon Hill says "Every adversity carries with it the seed of an equivalent or greater reward."

In Kemmer, Wyoming, fifty years ago there was a small western town of 1,500 population. Kemmer was the home and the opportunity of a young energetic man. He had big ideas that were germinated from the seed of a small store on Main Street. The resourceful man was J. C. Penney. Perhaps you are one of his customers. He had an idea and he wouldn't let go. Did you ever think of an idea? Did you ever try to? A fortune lies in unborn ideas, and ideas work through the brains of individuals just like you. It is this resourcefulness, the daring attitude that must be undertaken by the leaders in business.

A doctor friend of mine was having a problem collecting from his patients. At Christmas time, he decided he would write each one and cancel his bill. He also enclosed in the letter a card of regret that they had such a poor year financially! All but one paid his bill! That's being resourceful. The doctor could have sent a "stinging" letter, resulting in a strained relationship — perhaps anger and maybe the loss of a patient. Resourcefulness is the way you get results, by not doing the obvious.

There was a young man who got a job in a fish market in New York City. It was the city's largest fish market. This young man's job was to get the fish from the chute, carry it to a table and wrap it and pack it. The young man had only been working five days when the supervisor came to watch him work. After watching him for ten minutes he said, "I've been with this fish company twenty-seven years and you are wrapping and packing more fish than anyone ever has. How do you do it?" "It's very simple," the young man replied. "When I started to work here I was told what to do. After I did it a day or two, I decided to try to do a better, faster job. I knew you had been carrying the fish from the chute to the table since the company originated. What could I do? I just moved the wrapping table closer to the chute." A very simple thing like moving a table made the difference. He was resourceful, he was thinking, he was alive.

When Hitler was killing the Jews during the "heyday" of the Nazi regime, his Field Marshal Goering disagreed with him. One day the Field Marshal said, "I'm not in favor of your edict to kill the Jews, they are resourceful people and someday they could help you." He continued, "Come with me and let me show you what I mean." So Hitler followed the Field Marshall into a china shop that was operated by a German family. The Field Marshal said, "I would like to purchase a dozen left-handed tea cups." "I'm sorry," the German store owner said, "we don't have any." Now the Field Marshal took Hitler to a china shop operated by a Jewish family. "I'd like a dozen left-handed tea cups," said the Field Marshal. "Let me think a minute," said the Jewish store owner." "Oh yes, here they are, I just got a shipment in this morning." The Field Marshal and Hitler walked out of the store. "See what I mean?" said the Field Marshal. Hitler replied, "He was just lucky he got a shipment in this morning."

Resourcefulness is not just for the older person, the

businessman, the executive; it is for any age.

A young boy was selling orchids in Hawaii for $1.50 each. Now that doesn't seem like a lot of money, but please remember orchids grow in abundance in Hawaii. One Sunday at church a sales manager of a large company was amazed at the success this young boy was having selling orchids. He called the young boy over and said, "You are selling those orchids for $1.50 each and yet those same people could pick them wild down the road. How do you do it?" "Well sir," said the young boy, "when I approach a couple I look at the lady's fingers. If she is married I say to her, 'Would you like your boy friend to buy you an orchid?' If she not married, I say to the gentlemen, 'Would you like to buy your wife an orchid?' You see, mister, I've found out that those that are married wish they were not and those that aren't married wish they were."

How can I better myself and my condition? That is the basic question that will haunt you everyday of your life until you solve it. It starts with your own belief in yourself. You are entitled to all that is good. It is in the thinking in your mind that the wheels of accomplishment grind. There are no limitations — only those that you put on yourself. So don't let any enter your mind. The secret is to bring all your thoughts, your desires, aims and talents into the realm of your conscious mind. Open your mind to all that's good, being aware of the abundance at your command. Develop the mental attitude that it is rightfully yours to expect only the good. You have to believe in yourself if your business is to flourish, or if the boss is to "tap" you for the promotions. It is absolutely necessary for every man to believe in himself before he can be the person he wants to be. You've got to get up every morning with determination, if you are going to go to bed with satisfaction.

Success waits for you. Seize her, caress her — and she is yours. She belongs to you. Show no hesitation, for success is for the one who will master her.

How do we start? Ask yourself: what do I want from life?

Take the answer and nourish it. Do it right now. Let it become a part of you. Live as if it's becoming a reality. Believe that you have it. See yourself possessing it. Do this until you actually have it.

WIND THE CLOCK

We can hear a clock tick; we know why a clock ticks, but unless we wind the clock, nothing happens — it won't go.

This is one of life's greatest lessons: that nothing happens until we do it. We may know how we can be successful, we may have all the knowledge, but we must act, we must start, we must do it. No one else can wind us, no one else can start us, we must do it ourselves.

One of the greatest faults with people today is that their thirst for knowledge is present and they acquire it. They are intelligent, alert, receptive. In short, they have all the necessary credentials for success. You might say they are on the threshold of accomplishment. Yet something happens; they never utilize all the knowledge and intelligence that they have. They just don't "wind the clock" — they don't get started.

Remember, this is *your* clock! You are the only one who can wind it. Wind it well.

Our American heritage is to be a winner, to be successful, to do our best. Psychologists tell us that an inner feeling of success, of accomplishment, will make you a better person, a healthier person, a happier person, and, after all, these intangible results are what make life livable and you loveable.

Why will this be a great treasure to pass on?

In 90% of all families, if the parents are successful, the children will be successful! The patterns that one cultivates in his earliest years are most important and intelligent people have a tendency to develop these patterns in their children.

Eleanor Roosevelt said, "I do not waste my time in idleness and regret; too many people do. We totter and doddle, listening to everyone else's opinion and advice. We scurry around asking everybody what we should do, when the decision is within ourselves."

What we are doing is asking them to wind the clock. You have to wind it, and when you do, you will awaken a sleeping giant of courage. With this courage you will say, "Here I stand."

Above all, don't be afraid to step out. You are never alone. There is a hero of courage who will rise within you and face the problem.

There was a young fellow who answered a magazine advertisement, "How to Become a Taxidermist." He was anxious to learn the business and he enthusiastically waited for his course on taxidermy to arrive. To his surprise, they sent him a course on how to become a ventriloquist. He was disheartened, but as long as he had the instructions, he would try. He became quite good, and the neighbors encouraged him to follow a career as a ventriloquist.

One night while he was practicing he thought he should have a dummy. So he had his friend make him one. Now, he thought he'd better have a name for it — he called it Charlie McCarthy.

Do I need to say more? What did he do when his first obstacle appeared? He did the best he could with what he had to work with at that particular time.

Another young man was working in an office, making hardly enough to exist. His worldly possession consisted of nothing more than a dream. He dreamed of writing music. His only problem was he couldn't write it. He couldn't play an instrument, nor could he carry a tune. I believe you would agree, the odds were against this young man. Nevertheless, this young man kept writing lyrics, and a friend kept putting them to music. Then his big break came! He sold one of his songs — for 35c!

Two years later he sold another song — "Alexander's Rag Time Band" — did you ever hear of Irving Berlin?

Both Edgar Bergen and Irving Berlin found success, fame and fortune. They were like the clock on the wall. They heard the "ticking" inside of them, of a goal. They knew why there was a "ticking" inside, because they were enthusiastic they were determined to keep that "ticking" alive until they reached their goal.

There was another couple that must have kept their clock ticking. They were a shabby looking couple who pulled up one morning before the bank in a small town, in an old "flivver," that had weathered many winters. Alighting from the car, they entered the bank and approached the first teller, expressing their desire to purchase some war bonds. The teller, assuming by their dress and appearance that they had no money, directed them to the second teller. The second teller appraised the shabby couple and without any tact, sent them to the third teller. The third teller abruptly sent them to the president of the bank.

"How many bonds do you want?" asked the president.

"About $100,000 worth," the man replied.

"Do you have the money with you?" inquired the banker.

"Yep, it's out in the car in a big bucket," said the old man.

"Well, go get your money and we'll count it in the vault," said the president.

The old man and his wife went out to the car and returned, carrying a big bucket of money. They went to the vault and the banker began counting. After a while the banker looked up and said, "It's all here except $100.00."

When the old man heard that he turned to his wife and said, "Becky, I told you before we left home that you were getting hold of the wrong bucket."

I don't know how many buckets they had. I do know it took an effort to amass that fortune. I'm sure they were early risers, and that they worked hard. I'm equally certain they had a huge clock and they budgeted their time. I can visualize Becky winding the clock every day, as a sort of ritual. After all, what good is a clock if we don't wind it?

YOU CAN DO IT!

Why do some people succeed?

Andrew Carnegie started working for $4.00 per month. Later in life he became so wealthy he gave libraries to cities all over the world.

John D. Rockefeller became one of the richest men in the world; he started working for $6.00 a week.

Henry Ford started working for $2.50 per week.

Thomas Edison started as a newsboy on a train, and became the world's greatest inventor.

King Camp Gillette was born in a small town in Wisconsin. When he was seventeen his family had a fire and lost everything they had. So Gillette made his own way — ever hear of a safety razor?

Ulysses S. Grant failed as a businessman. At age 39 he was chopping wood for a living. Nine years later he was the President of the United States.

Why did these men succeed? The qualities that these men had, you have! Isn't that surprising?

Let's analyze this group of men. Not one had much education, so you can not blame your position in life on education. Not one of them had money in his family, so you can't use that as a reason for your position. Not one had a relative to give him a "break" in life. Now what are you thinking?

Every quality that made these men successful, you have. You have within you the same amount of faith, determination, ambition, desire, courage, and perseverance as they had. The only difference is they used these qualities, and they didn't know the meaning of the word "quit."

Do I mean that you can be just as successful today? Absolutely! Opportunities are just as prevalent today as yesterday.

We must remember that everything is changing — new

products, new businesses, and new methods. You are changing; you change a little everyday. This change can be for better or worse. You don't maintain your position, you go either forward or backward.

With all these changes, both around you and within you, new opportunities come to the top. The recognizing of these opportunities is the key to your success.

These men who succeeded in their fields were just like you. However, they utilized their inborn qualities and became successful.

Now the question is squarely up to you! Will you pay the price, will you work, will you be persistent, will you have faith?

Abraham Lincoln once said, "I know my opportunity will come and I shall be ready."

John Wesley, founder of the Methodist Church, asked a member of his church, who was mentally retarded, why a cow in the pasture was looking over the wall. The retarded man said, "Because he can't look through it." This is so true with our faults, our shortcomings and our bad habits. The secret is to look over them and forget them.

George Washington Carver, at the age of ten, was swapped as a slave for a horse worth $300.00. This remarkable young man overcame seemingly unsurmountable hardships to become a brilliant scientist. He is largely responsible for the development of the peanut industry. When asked how he attained such prominence and recognition, he said, "God Almighty works with me."

Some of you, reading about these individuals who made it with the odds stacked against them, will be like the farmer in this story.

This farmer and his wife were watching a parade in a rural country town. Now the farmer had seen parades before, but he had never seen a slide trombone. He was fascinated by it. He finally turned to his wife and, shaking his head, said, "He ain't a-foolin' me, he ain't a-swallowin' that."

PACKY

Packy East was born in Cleveland, Ohio. His ambition was to be a boxer — he was already a good amateur. However, in his first professional bout he was overmatched and took a terrible beating. He quit boxing and turned his attention to baseball, but he wasn't good enough to attract the attention of pro scouts. So he gave up his dream of being a big league baseball player.

Packy East left Cleveland and was not heard from. Years passed and people forgot Packy East.

The Cleveland Indians baseball club was sold to a group of men. The transaction ceremony was covered by the press, radio and TV. The man who was spokesman for the group purchasing the club was Packy East. Packy East, who had been forgotten, came back to buy the club he dreamed of playing with. Standing before the cameras tears ran down his face as he said, "Only in America can your dreams come true."

Now the name Packy East doesn't mean much to you, but his determination to make his dream come true is the thing to remember. Incidentally, Packy East's other name is Bob Hope.

Bob Hope has been a huge success in life. I'm discounting the money he's made. I'm thinking of how he has shared himself to make people happy all over the world. This is the true mark of a champion.

The experience that Bob Hope received in the ring and on the baseball field must have had a lasting effect on his entertainment career. He learned in athletics how to "take it" and carry on. He was intelligent enough to realize his future was not in baseball or boxing.

Too many people today will set a goal and not be versatile

enough to change to another goal if conditions aren't favorable for the original goal.

All our education, religion, and life itself, is built on going and growing to victory. I wouldn't give you 5c for a person who didn't want to win — one must win with honor or the winning is hollow.

Life doesn't determine a champion; a champion determines life. Life doesn't determine your success; you determine a successful life.

Bob Hope developed good pattern habits from his early athletic career. His career in the entertainment world wasn't handed to him. He had to battle just as hard. The difference was that he realized he was in his right profession. Once he was sure of this, he went full steam ahead to become one of the greatest and most respected comedians in the world.

I'm reminded of the story of a riverboat pilot. It seems that this pilot was talking to Mark Twain about steam replacing sails. The pilot was violently opposed to this new-fangled invention called the steam engine. Mark Twain, after listening to the outspoken pilot, finally said, "When it's steamboat time you steam."

Life does not stand still. Changes will be in order if you are to progress and be successful. It's your choice.

Of course you may be like the man who was asked if his wife had changed much since he married her. He replied, "Yes, she's changed my friends, my habits, and my hours."

Shortly after the turn of the century, a young fellow by the name of Bill was offered a contract to play with the Cincinnati Red Stockings. Bill was a good catcher and had dreamed of becoming a professional baseball player. When he was told the good news he ran home and related it to his father. His father angrily said, "No son of mine will be a professional baseball player. You are going to college." Bill was disappointed and went to his room to decide what he should do. He decided he would run away and join the Cincinnati Red Stockings. However, there was one last game to play with the local team before he left. In this last game Bill hurt his arm and was never able to play baseball again.

Bill took his father's advice and went to Yale University. He became a lawyer, just as his father wanted him to. Then he became a judge, just as his father had been. Then he became Chief Justice of the Supreme Court.

I relate this story to you to illustrate that sometimes things do not work out as we plan, that adjustments are in order. Then we reevaluate and do the most we can with what we have to work with at that time. Life doesn't always cater to our wishes. If we are to be successful, we must adapt ourselves to the best possible solution. Bill did just that. Bob Hope did the same.

All Bill's life he dreamed of being a baseball player and when the Cincinnati baseball club offered him nine hundred dollars, it seemed as though his dreams had come true. But tragedy struck and Bill had to forget his boyhood dream.

Bill had a good attitude, for he forgot his misfortune and applied himself to his studies and became an outstanding student. What I'm trying to make you understand is that Bill was not a quitter. He just reevaluated his life, then worked at his studies with the same intensity that he did with his baseball. He was successful at both.

How many times have we been disappointed and wanted to quit? How often have we had people that we counted on to let us down? We are going to have adversity come our way. We are all going to have to make a new start, climb another hill, look for another friend — just as Bill did. The secret of your success is, do you have what it takes, will you "pay the price," or will you quit?

Many years from now you might look back and say, "I reached my goal, I made my mark, I am successful." I know Bill said that for he became the twenty-sixth President of the United States — William Howard Taft.

If we always got everything we wanted, life would not be a challenge. The heartiest oaks grow where the elements are the most severe, where the wind or rain, sleet or snow test their very fibers everyday. A tree that is sheltered will not grow as sturdy as the oak does. We are a lot like a tree; if we are strong, we must be courageous and face the winds and rains of adversity.

Statistics tell us that 85% of all college graduates will change jobs within three years after graduation. Many times we take a position and may be satisfied, then an opportunity appears. The question is, do we have the courage to grasp that opportunity? This courageous step is the crux of all success: to act — to forget about the past, to burn your bridges behind you and go full steam ahead to your new opportunity.

"It isn't the size that makes the man, but how he thinks and how he plans."

HOPE

Many years ago a country doctor hitched his horse and wagon and walked into a drug store. He began talking to the clerk in a low tone. This meeting was destined to touch all corners of the globe and make many people wealthy. They talked for over an hour, never raising their voices above a whisper. Finally, the doctor went to his wagon and got a wooden paddle and a copper kettle and brought them into the store. The clerk inspected them and nodded in approval. He then reached in his pocket and pulled out $500.00, his life's saving. The doctor handed the clerk a piece of paper. On this paper was a formula that would start that kettle overflowing. What a fortune would flow!

So the next time you stop — whoever you are, wherever you are — for the "pause that refreshes," remember that's how Coca-Cola started. Think of the empire that grew out of the imagination of the clerk in the country drug store.

Imagination is the image of what we want. Imagination is one of our greatest assets; it is molded by past experience, education and environment. The young clerk had imagination and was glad to get the formula. For with this formula, imagination and hope, his new venture was off to a good start.

You need water, air and food, for without it you would die. But more important in life, you need hope! You need hope to face your dreams, to face opportunity, to make a decision or face a problem.

You need hope when you're young; when you're old and when you're breathing your last breath.

There is a Swedish proverb that says,

"Fear less, hope more, eat less, chew more; hate less, love more; and all good things are yours."

To make a better world for ourselves and others we look to

hope. There is nothing as powerful as hope. Without hope we die, with hope we live. With hope we dream, scheme, plan and work. With hope there is no quitting.

A boy in his first day of school was asked by his mother, "How did you like school?"

"I quit," he said.

"What do you mean, one day in school and you quit?"

He said, "I can't read, I can't write and the teacher won't let me talk. What's the use, I quit."

Without hope, you become a quitter. Speaking of being a quitter this teenage son was going to quit school. His dad said, "People who are remembered in life are those who never quit. Remember Henry Ford, Mickey Mantle, George Washington, and Thomas Edison? They never quit."

The father said, "And don't forget Percy Hamilton."

Boy replied, "Who's Percy Hamilton?"

Father said, "See you don't remember him, he quit."

If you have hope you will never quit, no matter what burdens you have to bear. So keep utmost in your mind that hope will be eternally with you, the beginning, middle and end of your life.

Without hope you have no lever over problems, illness, despair and temporary setbacks. Regardless of your confrontation, with hope your dreams will grow, opportunities will be seized and problems solved.

What is hope? Perhaps a figment of the mind. A deep-seated feeling that keeps gnawing away. A feeling that says, "I will." A feeling that keeps spurring us on when the odds seem heavy against us. It is a feeling that turns a depressed, discouraged, despondent person into a happy, courageous, goal-setting individual.

For it is hope, whatever it is, whoever it is, that gives us the sparkle, the glow, the energy to keep us grasping, stretching, reaching for something just beyond our reach, and even if we never reach our chosen goal we will be better for having tried. This is the mark of a person with hope.

THE REAL FORTUNE

Some work hard all their lives
For things they'll never get,
And when the Master calls they
Leave with deep regret.

They were constantly searching
For something, so they said,
And they were still a-looking
When the doctor said, "They're dead."

Their goal was to amass a fortune
As time went stealing by.
They were sure with perseverance
They'd find their "pie in the sky."

A lesson we should remember:
Real fortunes can come true,
But you must awaken them
For they're fast asleep in you.

—Roy Pinyoun

OPPORTUNITY

Sir Walter Raleigh was a writer, patriot, revolutionary and statesman. Did you know that? When we think of Sir Walter Raleigh we remember him as the man who spread his cloak over a mud puddle so the queen could walk across the street.

What did Sir Walter Raleigh do? He used imagination, and he acted. He decided what had to be done and he did it.

Plan your work and work your plan, is known to all salesmen. Know what you're going to do and do it.

A lady went to a lecture one night and the speaker said, "Take advantage of opportunity." She went home and could not undo her buttons. She thought: opportunity — that's it; I'm going to invent a button that will be easy to undo. She invented "snap buttons."

What did this lady do? She used imagination and she acted. How many other women had the same problem undoing buttons and did nothing about it?

Everything starts from thoughts, and you can think. Your "thinking machine" is greater than any computer. Your brain has four billion units of information, compared to a computer that has four million units. Do you know the difference between a million and a billion? Let's use $1,000 bills as an example. A stack of $1,000 bills one foot high would be a million dollars. How high would the stack be to make a billion dollars? As high as the Washington Monument in Washington, D.C.

What does it take to be a leader? We know we must have imagination and action; we must also have an abundance of energy, drive and ambition. These are the qualities that put the driver in the driver's seat.

The key to successful companies is the leadership up front.

I'd rather have a flock of lambs led by a tiger than a pack of tigers led by a lamb.

Regardless of our niche, we must be suitably trained to fill our role. I would rather have a well-trained mediocre man than a half-trained superior man. This again is the barometer of a well-managed organization, for there is no substitute for knowledge or training.

It seems that a mother was watching men tar the road in front of her house. They were spreading the watery, tarred substance that is used for sealing purposes. She was explaining to her five year-old son what they were doing.

All of a sudden, the five year-old son breaks away from his mother's grasp and runs out in the street. The young boy slipped and rolled over in this sticky, tarry mess. Picking himself up, he made his way back to his mother. The mother looked at the little boy and said, "I'd rather have another, than clean and re-train this one."

The blessing bestowed upon us is: all that we need to be successful is free — ours for the asking. Do you know where it is? It's within you; recognize this and use it. All of these blessings, coupled with a positive attitude and faith, are unbeatable; it's your design for success. So count your blessings and use them.

Speaking of the positive, it seems that two men were shipwrecked, and in time their raft came within sight of a tropical island. One man, expecting the worst said, "I'll bet it's inhabited by a bunch of wild men." The other man said, "Cheer up, pal. Where there are wild men, there are wild women."

Above all, in times of sorrow, in times of happiness, in times of defeat, in times of victory — have faith! We should remember that faith is the "Ark" during our flood of troubles, and prayer is the rudder that will guide our "Ark."

The greatest mystery to me is that some of us only turn to God in time of sorrow when it appears all is lost. God is for always! Now, today, "ask and ye shall receive; knock and the door shall be opened."

There is a story of a little girl crawling onto her Daddy's knee and saying, "Daddy, why can't Mommy and I have new dresses for church like Becky and her mother? I ask God every night to help you, so you'll be successful, but he doesn't seem to hear me 'cause he doesn't help you." The Father held her tight so she wouldn't see the tears. Finally, he said, "Kathy, honey, you and Mommy will get new dresses, 'cause God wants to help Daddy. The problem is, Daddy isn't asking God."

There were two girls running to get to school on time. One girl said, "Let's stop and pray that we won't be late." The other girl replied, "Let's pray and keep running."

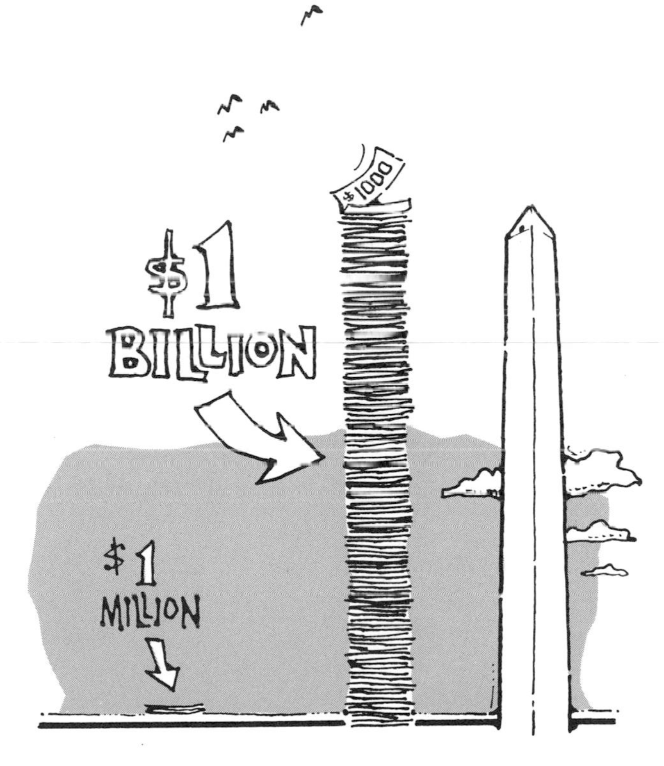

THE DOOR OPENS

We sometime think that life's unfair,
As we face our daily task.
That fate has over-burdened us
With things we'd never ask.

If we would stop and be grateful,
And take the time to pray,
To know that all we seek in life
Can't possibly come our way.

That we must have our heartaches,
And disappointments too,
But we should keep our faith alive
In all the things we do.

Remember God is ever-present;
As close as any mother.
And everytime a door He closes,
He opens up another.

—Roy Pinyoun

THE ECHO

In 1903 some angry miners ignited a carload of coal and pushed it down a mine shaft. For the next fifty years it burned, consuming ten million tons of coal, covering an area of ten square miles. It has been rumored that neighboring farmers complained about their potatoes being cooked when they were yet in the ground.

Ever since our early history we have been trying to solve our problems through hate. In reality we fail to realize that the direct opposite is true.

One day a mother spanked her little son, and he went screaming out of doors. "I hate you — hate you — hate you," he cried at the top of his lungs. Back from a cliff across the way bounced the youngster's words, clear and distinct, "I hate you — hate you — hate you." The little fellow scrambled back into the house and cried, "Mother, someone out there hates me." The mother took her son by the hand and led him back outdoors. "Now," she said, "son, yell this, I love you — love you — love you." The boy yelled the words. Back from the cliff clear and distinct came the echo, "I love you — love you — love you." This is a law of life, my boy; what we give, we get back in return. Love answers every human need and always will.

Speaking of love, I'm reminded of the young man who was riding horseback with his girlfriend. As they stopped to rest, the two horses rubbed necks affectionately. "Ah, me," said the lad, "that's what I'd like to do too." "Go ahead," said the girl, "It's your horse."

THE HAPPY MAN

His clothes were a little ragged, and faded too.
His shirt was a bit out of style.
He'd walk down the street whistling a tune,
On his face he carried a smile.

T'was a pleasure to see him walking along
Greeting the folks that he'd meet
And everyone loved the little old man
Who had hardly enough to eat.

He had love in his heart for everyone,
The Master had found his soul,
He had discovered the beauty of life.
Spreading happiness, that was his goal.

And when he passed on, and folks gathered round
To bury the man who was poor,
They found he had given his suit away
To someone who needed it more.

—Roy Pinyoun

PERFECT

Driving from Tulsa to Oklahoma City in the summer of 1975, I decided to stop at a country store which had a large sign advertising delicious apples for sale. There was a huge barrel of big, red, fat apples. I bought a bag, jumped in my car, anticipating how wonderful they were going to taste. Later, as I looked in the bag and discovered there wasn't a big, red, fat apple there, I was angry. I would have gone back but I was now twenty-five miles down the road. It occurred to me that the grocer had a few good apples on the top. When he filled my bag, he had reached below and given me the little ones. As I calmed down, I wondered — had the grocer deliberately given me these inferior apples. Of course not; it is when the barrel is shaken that the big red, fat apples always come to the top, and the small ones sink to the bottom.

As shaking the barrel brings the best to the top, could it be that we are all apples in the barrel of life and in the future the best will come to the top? This barrel is shaking all the time — in business, in athletics, on television, you name it, and it's shaking. So, if we're foolish enough to think that by being placed in a top position we will stay there, perish the thought for at the first shaking, we'll be back on the level we deserve.

If we have small desires, we will remain small. If we have great desires, we can become great. It's all in where we place our values.

For weeks the couple had gone from showroom to showroom as the husband looked at new autos. He just could not make up his mind. "My, how you've changed," his wife chided him. "You married me three weeks after you saw me." "I know," he said impatiently, "but buying a car is serious business."

Earl Nightingale says, "Success is the progressive realization of a worthy ideal.'' He doesn't say you have to make a great deal of money. If you want to be the best school teacher, or operate the finest service station, or be the best butcher, these are all worthy ideals. It's where you place your values. A good school teacher is just as happy as a successful executive who may earn ten times the teacher's salary.

When I was in the drive-in business, I had the best handyman working for me that anyone could have. He did his job to perfection, and was happy in what he was doing — he was successful. Perhaps there wasn't anyone else working for me who would do William's work. However, to William it was the perfect job. Perfection is in the eyes of the beholder.

A little boy went to a large department store to buy his mother a birthday present. He finally decided he would buy a blouse. When the clerk asked the little boy what size, the boy replied, ''I don't know except she's perfect!'' The clerk wrapped a size 36 blouse. The following day, the boy's mother brought the blouse back to exchange for another size. The little boy knew his mother was perfect in his eyes, but she wore a size 48 blouse.

AS WE THINK

There is an ancient Greek proverb, "As a man thinketh, so he is." This is the key to an abundant life.

The difference between the successful and unsuccessful one is in the way one looks at things. It is not a matter of preparation. It isn't whether you were lucky or whether opportunity came along.

The successful person seizes opportunity, disregarding what the outcome may be. He just recognizes opportunity and visualizes what he can do with it. He completely eliminates failure from his thoughts.

The unsuccessful person sees the same opportunity and wants to take advantage of it but doesn't. He fills his mind with all the reasons why he can't.

Nearly everyone I know, and I'm sure you will agree, at one time had opportunity smiling at them but were powerless to act. The famous sad and frightening words, "If I had only taken that chance," has been said by all of us at some time or other.

It's all in your thinking!

There is a story about a little old lady who lived by herself. The fact that she was eighty-two did not keep her from spending many hours each day working in her yard. Her yard was the prettiest on the street. At the age of eighty-four she was stricken with polio and was confined to her wheel chair. The neighbors helped her to make the adjustment to life in a wheel chair. One day one of the neighbors visited her and without thinking said, "I guess when you are stricken with polio, it colors your life." The little old lady looked up and said, "Yes, it does color one's life; but I'm so fortunate, I select the colors."

Your thoughts can make you or break you. Your mental attitude attracts good or bad, whatever you decide. We can do what we want to do, have what we want to have, and be what we want to be. What we do, what we have and what we are depends on our thinking.

There is the story of Napoleon's young drummer boy. One day Napoleon went up to the young boy and said, "Lad, can you play everything we may need on your drum?" The young boy of fourteen looked up and said, "I can't play Retreat and I am not going to learn."

The secret is to start something. Give your mind a little exercise and start it working on something constructive. The greatest success secret is to create, be creative. Perhaps it won't come easy, so force yourself, drive yourself, release the pent up energy and start your motor. Then keep driving until you reach your achievement.

When your achievements or triumphs occur is not important, nor should they impress others. You might only have built your first table, or constructed your first greenhouse. This might not impress others — so what! All that counts is your own opinion of what you've done, of your own achievement.

For the person who recognizes his own abilities and utilizes them there is no goal that can't be reached. With the achievement of one goal, the steps to the next become easier. As this continues, success becomes a habit and you make a habit of success.

Everyone must set his own goal. One young man had a goal, but I don't recommend it. He got a job working for a contractor digging a ditch for a sewer line. The contractor said, "I'll pay you $2.00 per hour and you'll work eight hours a day." The young man agreed, picked up the shovel and started to dig. Sometime later the contractor came to see how the young man was doing. To his surprise the young man was sitting under a tree and another man was digging the ditch. The contractor said to the young fellow he had hired, "I don't understand, why aren't you digging the ditch?"

The young fellow replied, "I hired him to work for me."

"What are you paying him," asked the contractor?

"Two dollars an hour," he replied.

"Then you're not making any money." said the contractor.

"I know," said the young fellow, "but I'm boss."

Almost everyone wants to be boss. The important thing is to be boss of yourself; to be boss with a positive attitude.

There were twin boys born to a wealthy family. One of the boys at the age of twelve was timid, cautious, and negative in all his thinking and actions. The other was the direct opposite, outgoing, courageous, with a positive approach to everything he did. This concerned the parents, so they took both boys to a psychiatrist. The psychiatrist decided he would try an experiment. Several days later he asked the timid boy to go up to his room and do whatever he wanted to do. The boy went upstairs to his bedroom and to his surprise the room was filled with every toy imaginable. The boy looked at all the toys and then sat down on the side of his bed. The psychiatrist and parents had been watching; but to see the boy just sitting on the bed and not playing with the toys was too much. They entered the room and the psychiatrist said, "Why are you not playing with the toys?"

The boy replied, "I'm afraid if I do I might break one and mother would scold me."

The next day they said to the other son, "Go out to the room by the barn and close the door." He immediately went out to the room near the barn that was filled with manure. Through a window the psychiatrist and the parents observed the boy. To their amazement he had a pitch fork and was pitching the manure from one side to the other. They opened the door and the father said, "Son, what are you doing?"

The son replied, "With all this manure there has to be a pony somewhere."

Hard work, constructive thinking and a positive attitude — all lead up to achievement. As we achieve, we continue achieving and this becomes our pattern of life, our success pattern.

Perhaps we can sum it up by this story.

A young fellow gets a job in a lead mine, it is his first job and he is full of enthusiasm. As he approaches the supervisor on this first day, he says, "How can I become successful?"

The supervisor smiles and says, "By getting the lead out!"

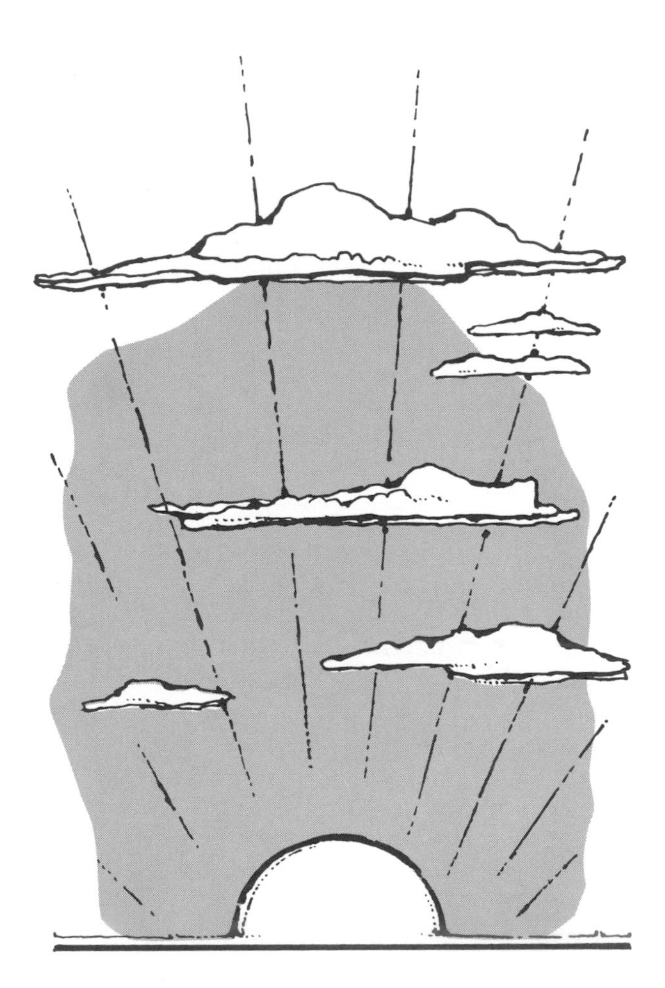

SOCRATES

Socrates, the great philosopher, was asked by a young boy, "Sir, I would like to learn with you." Socrates said, "Follow me." The great philosopher took the young boy to the river and shoved him in the water. Then Socrates jumped in and sat on the young boy. The young boy struggled, but to no avail. Socrates continued to hold the boy under the water. Finally, after swallowing water and choking, the boy made one last effort to get out of the clutches of Socrates. With this last effort he managed to free himself and crawl out of the water. After getting his breath, he said to Socrates "What were you trying to do, drown me?" Socrates made his famous reply, which has been passed down through the ages: "This is how much I want you to want to learn with me."

Socrates taught this boy a lesson that we can all learn from — that success is going to be in direct proportion to the effort put forth. It doesn't matter whether you're pushing a wagon or reading a book, the direct result is going to be the result of the intensity of this effort.

Too many people today are getting by by using as little effort as possible. This may be hindering the company they're working for and it most certainly is hindering their promotion schedule. Yet, some people enjoy giving the employer just half effort. However, in the final analysis the loser is the person who gives the half effort.

My father used an expression that has stayed with me for many years. "Do what you're paid to do and 'then some.' It's the 'then some' that gets your salary raised." I think this sums things up.

Psychologists tell us that we use approximately 15% of our innate ability and that 85% is never used. Did it ever occur to you how you could surpass your competitors if you would just give a 25% effort?

There is a thin line between success and failure. A thin line between winning and losing. That thin line is the extra effort, the extra 10%. Do you want to be a little better? Do you want to be a little more successful? Will you pay the price? Will you give a little extra?

Your grandparents told your parents and your parents have told you that there is a right and wrong way of doing things. What they have probably not told you is that there is a right and wrong way of doing the right thing.

Socrates knew this! He knew the young boy was sincere, but he wanted intensified effort. Socrates was like the famous orchestra leader who walked into rehearsal and waved his hands for silence. "Now gentlemen, the opening of this symphony must be played softly, very, very softly. It opens like a whisper. Now!" The men prepared themselves, the leader raised his baton and before a note was played he lowered his baton. "No, no gentlemen, it's too loud." He was reaching for the impossible, but he made his point.

The basis of all democracy is that man is not bound by any system, that he need not accept the world the way he finds it, but may arrange it according to his own ideas. It is only the raw material. He can do with it what he wills. It is the new idea that is responsible for all inventions, all progress. You should be satisfied with nothing. More than ever, right now, new ideas are remaking the very world you live in. Emerson in his wonderful essay on "Experience" says: "Dream delivers us to dream and there is no end to illusion. Life is a train of moods like a string of beads, and as we pass through them they prove to be many colored lenses which paint this world their own hue and each shows only what lies in *its* focus."

Fran Tarkington, quarterback for the New York Giants, was asked, "How are you able to quarterback the Giants to so many victories?" Fran replied, "I carry an image of victory in my heart."

A successful life does not result from chance but from a succession of successful days. Your body's growth is from food, but your success in life comes from within. This growth from within is so essential, for without it we start to die.

THE AUCTION

The devil was having an auction. He was auctioning off blocks, and each block he was selling had a name on it. There was envy, hate, malice, jealousy, and many others. There was a wedge-shaped block he would not sell, it was called discouragement. When the devil was asked why he would not sell it, he replied, "This one block called discouragement is all I need to control people. If I can just use this wedge-shaped block I can stop progress. I can shove this block into the lives of people and make them unhappy with their lives. It has so many uses, that I feel I can get by successfully by just this one block of discouragement. It fits into everyone's life. The market is enormous. I've been successful and I'm sure I'll continue to be successful with it."

Discouragement is the knife that cuts the ropes of all your dreams, ambitions, desires and ideas. It's the force that stops the flow of accomplishment. It's the tap that drains your energy, when removed. It is all around you; it's ever-present. It's yours for the using; it's free. It's a deadly pestilence; it's a worm and it should be stepped on. If you don't kill it, it could kill you.

Dr. Charles Stine held the prestigious position of being Director of Chemical Products of Du Pont Company. In 1928, after being with Du Pont for twenty-one years he personally recommended Dr. Wallace Carothers to be in charge of the Research Department.

Carothers was then thirty-one years old and recognized as one of the potentially great minds in the country. He had a difficult personality, impatient, nervous, and thin-skinned. However, his scientific knowledge gained everyone's admiration.

In 1935 he created one of the happiest and most exciting times in the Du Pont history. He announced he was on the verge of perfecting nylon. With a team of over 200 experts, they were given the go-ahead to commercialize Carothers discovery. In 1938, three years later, Du Point announced to the world the practicality of nylon. It is estimated that $29,000,000 was invested before the first pound of nylon was sold.

What happened to the inventor? What rewards did Wallace Carothers receive? He killed himself! Dr. Wallace Carothers, just before the "break through," had become a heavy drinker, highly nervous and unstable. He did not have the courage to carry on when the goal was in sight. He never knew of the product he created — a creator who was unable to face the creation.

The devil was more persistent than Carothers, he waited with his wedge — discouragement.

Have you heard the story of the man who arrived at the Pearly Gates and requested St. Peter to let him in? "How are you qualified for Heaven?" asked St. Peter. The man replied, "I never drank, I never smoked, I never lost my temper, I never went with women!" St. Peter said, "Wait a minute. I'm not interested in what you didn't do. I'm interested in what you did do."

There are many prerequisites to success, the courage to start and the courage to finish. It is estimated that 85% of the people will never start anything original. Of the 15%, 9% see it through to completion. You can never get anything completed if you don't start and you are foolish to start if you don't intend to finish. You're "spinning your wheels," you're not going anywhere. You're like the man who was going "to start to commence" to begin tomorrow.

If you want to live a dull, drab, tame life, then don't start to look for the future. If you want to be the average guy with the average car and the average home, then don't dream, don't plan and don't start. But if you want to climb mountains, if you want to look for wide horizons, then dream big dreams. When you do, put all the energy into it that you can muster, and see it through to completion. Always looking for your rainbow.

If you're the person I think you are, you'll climb those mountains and you'll reach your horizons and you'll make your dreams come true. As for your rainbow — it will color your life with the thrilling, exciting feeling of satisfaction. This can only be yours if you have the courage to start!

The principle ingredients in successful accomplishments are: the courage of "come what may" variety, and the capacity for hard work. Theodore Roosevelt once said, "I'm just an ordinary fellow, but I work at it more than most ordinary men." When Winston Churchill was asked to speak at Harrow, the school he attended as a young man, he said, "You have asked me to speak to you this morning on the necessary ingredients for success. There are many," he continued, "However, the advice I'm going to give you this morning can be summed up in one sentence. Whatever you do in life — never quit, never, never, never!"

I'm reminded of the story of the town drifter who got a job at a railroad siding. His job was to remove golf carts from the boxcar. He was warned that he should keep the brake on so that the carts would roll slowly down the incline. On Friday afternoon, his fourth day on the job, three golf carts went racing down the incline and into a huge oil pit — he had forgotten to put the brakes on. The manager came running from his office with anger written all over his face. The town drifter held up his hand and said, "You need not come mouthing me, because I've left."

There is a price tag on everything you do — everything costs something, and eventually you'll have to pay the price. People who are successful know this and do not avoid paying. The losers are those who do not want to pay the price; they are looking for the easy way out.

If you want to be a lawyer, your price is education; a doctor, it is the same. If you aspire to be a good baseball player, your price is practice, practice, practice. This applies to golf, tennis, and so many sports where hard work many times surpasses ability.

With all our government hand-outs, some people are forgetting how to give and how to work, they just want to take.

Speaking of "taking," that reminds me of the maid who worked for a wealthy family. She had her large handbag and was walking out the side-door to catch the bus. The lady of the house said, "Mary, would you please go and tidy up the two bathrooms? I'm having company over tonight." The maid left her handbag and went into the house to do the cleaning. The lady decided she'd look in Mary's handbag. When she did she found an unopened five pound bag of sugar. She took the five pounds of sugar and put it back in the kitchen. Mary finished her work, picked up her bag and left. The next day Mary didn't show up for work. The lady of the house called Mary and asked, "Mary, why didn't you come to work today?" Mary replied, "I don't work for people who steal back."

PERSISTENCE

A young fellow got a summer job working for the Standard Oil Company. It was the first job he ever had.

It is customary for oil companies to have contests to see who can sell the most of a certain product. In the summer time they usually encourage the sale of car polish and wax. The reason is that people wax and wash their car more often in the summer time.

This particular contest was for sixty days, to determine who could sell the most polish and wax. At the conclusion of the contest, a young fellow won who had never had a full time job before. The supervisor came by and asked the young fellow, "How did you win the contest, when you have had no selling experience? You didn't know any of the customers; in fact, you were competing against men who did. Besides, you were competing against men who have been in the business many years." The young man hesitated a moment and then said, "I knew we had the best wax and polish on the market, I know because I tried it. Then I didn't ask every other person if they wanted to buy the best polish and wax on the market; I didn't just ask some of the people, I asked everyone!"

He was persistent. He asked everyone. How important this is to be persistent. The older, more seasoned workers thought that they could determine who would buy the products by looking at them, or their car. This is so true about salesmen today.

The biographies of great men will tell you that success came after a temporary set-back. Not always, but many times — and it is being persistent that turns the temporary set-back into success. The minute you are not persistent you are defeated. It's a personal matter; it's up to you and only you. No one can be persistent for you.

It's like the young lady who was in love with three young men and didn't know which one to marry. One day she called her three lovers together and said, "I love you all, but I must decide which one I want to marry. So I've decided that I'm not going to marry any of you for thirty days. During this period of thirty days you may spend ten dollars on a gift for me. At the end of this time I'll marry one of you." The first young man decided to buy a picture that she could hang in her living room. He rationalized that every time she looked at the picture she would think of him. The second young man decided he would buy her a dog. He thought the pet would constantly remind her of him. The third young man went to the Western Union office and inquired of the price of a telegram. With his ten dollars he could send her ten telegrams, which he did. So every three days she got a telegram that read, "I love you, I love you, I love you!" Who do you think the young lady married? — the persistent one. When this young lady decided to get married, she wanted to become the perfect mate, and learn to do everything he could do. First, she had to learn to drive, so she took the beginning instructions. However, because of all the showers and parties, she was unable to complete her driving course. The only permit she could get was the beginners permit. The wedding over and all the festivities completed, they were off on their honeymoon. A few minutes later, everyone was amazed to see the young bride come running excitedly into the house. "Oh dear," she said, "I almost spoiled everything, I drove off without my beginners permit."

GOALS

When I think of goals, I think of the inmate who was sitting up against a tree watching the grass grow. A farmer passed by the inmate who, being a friendly fellow, said, "Hi there, friend. What do you do for a living?" "I'm a farmer," was the reply. "Is that so," said the inmate, "I've done a bit of farming myself. Too much work for me; I quit." "By the way," the inmate went on; "have you ever tried being crazy?" "Certainly not," answered the farmer. "Well, you should," said the inmate, "it's got farming beat comin' and goin'."

I guess we could say the farmer and the inmate both had goals. The farmer wanted to be a good farmer and the inmate wanted to be the best inmate. Seems like they were doing a job of it.

Everything about us had to start with a dream, a desire, a wish, a goal, a definite major purpose. It didn't just happen. It had to start within someone's mind. You have to visualize it as a completed task. After you have visualization, you must go into activating; you must develop your thought to completion by doing one job at the time.

Nothing is as powerful, encouraging and enjoyable as a goal whose time has come, and nothing is as sad, important and dead as a goal that has been laid to rest. Too many people go to their graves with their goals still within them.

Can you imagine what a basketball game would be without a goal, or a football game, a hockey or soccer game? The goal is necessary for achievement. If we didn't have a goal on the basketball floor the men would just run around accomplishing nothing. As soon as you hang a goal, there's a purpose. Of course, the players would get exercise, without a goal, but it would become boring.

Now, let's look at our lives without a goal. Of course,

you'd go to work, come home, eat and in all probability watch TV. You might say that would be good — but would it? Would you like to work at that job without a future for thirty years? Would you like to wonder how your children are going to go to college? Do you want to live in the same house and drive the same car year after year? Of course you don't!

To me, and I'm sure you'll find the same answer, the important thing in life is the satisfaction of achievement — the reaching of a goal — the inner feeling of winning, of knowing that you were able to drive yourself to victory. This need not be a big victory, but the first of a series of victories. Each time you win, you're a better person outwardly and inwardly.

We are not going to win all the time; this, too, is a barometer of how much you want to be a winner. Where you fail — there are one of two things that is going to happen. You are going to quit, or you are going to be more determined than ever. The secret is to get up when you fall down.

A young man was walking down the street in San Antonio, Texas, many years ago. He was hungry, he was dirty, he was tired, he was broke, and a sheriff was looking for him for not paying his room rent. As he walked along the street on this hot, sultry summer day, he saw a morning newspaper in a trash can. He picked up the paper and noticed on the front page a picture of the Waldorf Hotel opening in New York. The Waldorf, the largest hotel in the world! It had two thousand rooms, eating facilities to feed twenty-five thousand at one time, a hundred dish washers were employed, five hundred waiters, and a hundred cooks. This was the Waldorf opening in New York.

As this young man read the paper, he tore out the picture of the Waldorf, folded it four times and put it in his shirt pocket. As he did, he said, "Someday that will be mine." Seventeen years later, he bought it for twenty-seven million dollars. His name was Conrad Hilton, owner of the vast chain of Hilton Hotels. Conrad Hilton was a dreamer, and he made his dream come true. He had a dream and he wouldn't let go.

Conrad Hilton took seventeen years to complete his "dream" but it had to start within him. He never forgot what his ultimate dream was, but it took years to grow, years to accumulate the necessary money and know-how to make his dream come true. The picture that he tore out of the paper is now framed and it hangs on his office wall. The picture of the Waldorf became part of him, an obsession, a goal. He wanted it so much that he eventually was able to purchase it.

A goal that you visualize must be conceivable, achievable, and believable; you must be realistic. It must be something in the realm of possiblity. Conrad Hilton was able to purchase the Waldorf because he started by buying and constructing smaller hotels first. He continued to grow. Then, with financial assistance and the proper personnel, he achieved his most treasured goal — he bought the Waldorf. He set small goals along the way, each small goal a stepping stone to his long-term goal.

He believed he could some day own the Waldorf. He honestly believed it. It was believable. He thought it was conceivable. It was quite a goal but in his mind he thought it possible. It was conceivable. Perhaps the best way to sum it up is with the words of Napoleon Hill: "What the mind of man can conceive and believe, it can achieve."

Edison dreamed of an incandescent light bulb, Hannibal dreamed of crossing the Alps, and Henry Ford dreamed of a "horseless carriage." Their dreams all came true. They made their dreams a reality. They wouldn't quit. People laugh at the dreamer because they don't dream. People laugh at his trying because they don't try, and they'll laugh at his spirit for they don't understand.

We live in the present. We dream of the future, and most important, we learn from the past. These men were all dreamers, but more than that, they were prepared for the hardships. They were mentally prepared.

A person must be prepared or he'll be like the marine who

was following two girls. Finally, one of the girls turned around and said, "You either quit following us or get another sailor."

In closing, hang up your goals and play life's game. Play the game, so that when your playing days are over, you can sit back and say, "I did my best. I tried. I really tried."

THE TIGERS

I'm sure you've seen gyms in the larger cities where fighters work and prepare for their upcoming fight. Along the side of the gym are punching bags, both the light and heavy ones. Most days you can find boxers skipping rope, shadow boxing or going through a series of exercise maneuvers to develop their body. Everyone has the same dream — to become a champion.

This particular day there was a young fellow in the ring, boxing against a worthy opponent. He was quick, he had a good left jab, a fine right cross and could roll with the punches. His manager, trainer, and backers were excited; they were visualizing a championship, money, and fame.

Sitting across the ring was the Old Timer, his nose was pushed to the right, the result of his too-long ring career. He had cauliflower ears and scars that etched his face, telling the story of overmatched fights. He was not a wealthy man, but he was wealthy in ring knowledge and experience.

The manager, trainer and backers went over to the Old Timer and with enthusiasm asked, "Isn't he great, doesn't he have a good left jab, and a right cross; doesn't he roll with the punches?" The "Old Timer" didn't say anything; he shifted a cigar he was chewing from one side of his mouth to the other. Finally he looked up and said, "I'll let you know how good he is after he's been knocked down. Man, like a tree, is best measured after he has been knocked down." It doesn't matter how many times you're knocked down — what matters is how fast you get up.

Jack Dempsey, former world heavyweight champion was asked why college graduates don't make good fighters. Dempsey replied, "They're too smart — the fight game is the toughest game on earth. When I was a young fighter I was knocked down plenty. I wanted to stay down, but I couldn't

— I needed that extra $2.00 for finishing on my feet. I was one of those hungry fighters. When you haven't eaten in two days, you understand. In one of my early fights, I was knocked down eleven times before I got up and won." He continued, "Do you think I would have gotten up if I had money? No," said Dempsey, "college graduates never get that low."

I've always had the utmost admiration for boxers; the courage they have to enter the ring, and face their opponents, whose goal is to literally destroy them.

Many centuries ago there was a similar situation. It was during Caesar's reign when he was trying to conquer the world. During one of his campaigns his Army encountered a small country called Ireland. Ireland didn't have much of an army, but the soldiers they had were tough. Caesar's generals reported this to him. Caesar said, "Select their two strongest, most courageous soldiers and bring them to me." On Monday morning, two of Ireland's toughest men stood before Caesar. Caesar said, "Gentlemen, I am told you are brave and good fighters. We shall give you your opportunity next Saturday night at the Circus we will have in the Coliseum. You will fight ten of my strongest gladiators. After the fight is over we will give you a nice burial." On that Saturday night the two Irishmen beat Caesar's gladiators beyond recognition. On Monday morning Caesar had the two Irishmen come before him. "Gentlemen," said Caesar, "you have showed us all that you can fight, and I congratulate you for it. However, next Saturday night at the Coliseum you will face ten gladiators — this time they will be on horses and carry spears. So I assure you, again, that after Saturday night we will give you a nice burial." On Saturday night the Irishmen again gave the gladiators a sound beating and broke their spears over their heads. Monday morning Caesar met the Irishmen and said, "You are indeed talented fighters and I congratulate you. However, next Saturday night you will face sixty man-eating tigers in the Coliseum. Again, I will promise you a nice burial." The next Saturday morning the two Irishmen are sitting in the Coliseum where they could hear the tigers growling. Finally Mike said, "Terrance, did I hear voices in your cell last night or was I dreaming?" "No," replied Terrance, "They were voices. I meant to tell you. Do you remember the first Saturday in the Coliseum when that pretty young girl smiled at me and threw me a flower? Well, that Saturday, when we defeated the gladiators who were on horses she sent me a note that said she was coming to see me. Mike, she came last night — she bribed the guards and brought me wine and food. We drank the wine and she said nice things to me. Then I said nice things to her. She cuddled up close to me and I held her tight." "Yes, yes, Terrance, then what happened?" "Mike, I want to tell you the whole story but you'll have to wait — I hear the tigers coming."

Courage and confidence, what a team!

THE KING OF THE JUNGLE

There was a steamboat owner who wanted to take his boat down the Ohio River. He interviewed numerous pilots and finally met one who said, "I know every sandbar in the Ohio River." And that he did for he grounded the boat on the first turn!

After getting the boat afloat again, the owner hired another pilot who said, "I may not know where all the sandbars are, but I know exactly where the channel is." He made the trip without any problems.

This second pilot did not dwell on the sandbars, currents, dangers, and what he shouldn't do. He kept a true course in the channel, doing what was right. Right will always win out if you have faith. Of course this pilot had grounded boats — he had misjudged the currents and made mistakes, but he had learned.

One of the secrets of life is to get up when you fall down. This is the successful approach — it's part of the learning process. Every time you get up, you've succeeded — "You're a winner."

There are many people today who start out in life determined that they'll succeed, that they'll be a winner, until the first big obstacle hits them. Then they quit.

They are like the lion that lived in the jungle. One day he thought it was time to remind everyone that he was still King of the Jungle. The first animal he saw was the gorilla.

"Who is King of the Jungle?", he asked. "You are, great lion," the gorilla replied. Then he saw a tiger and said, "Tiger, who is King of the Jungle?" "You are, great lion," said the tiger. Next he met an elephant and said, "Who is the King of the Jungle?" The elephant picked the lion up with his trunk, slammed him against the ground, stomped him a couple of times and threw him in the lake. The lion came out of the water, shook himself a few times and said to the elephant, "Just because you don't know the answer, *don't get mad.*"

COURAGE

Everyday, everywhere, somehow people are being asked to call on their courage to answer some critical situation. Courage is a dynamic force, it is the light in life, where there are pain, problems, discouragement and failure. Courage is the quality within individuals that shows itself in times of decision, danger and opposition. It is the thirst to do what is necessary, always with a positive approach, which in itself is the passport for a better tomorrow.

When I think of courage at its pinnacle I think of Three Rivers, Quebec. Three Rivers is a sleepy town spreading itself along the shores of the narrow, but treacherous, St. Lawrence River. The city, with its French Canadian population, thrives on its paper industry. Its ornate buildings crowd the narrow streets giving one the feeling of being in ancient France. Its massive and numerous cathedrals stand majestically, demonstrating the religious atmosphere of the city.

While playing professional baseball with the Three Rivers' team, I met the incredible Pete Gray. Pete Gray was born in Nanticote, Pennsylvania. He was twenty-three years old, six feet tall and weighed 177 pounds. Pete was center fielder, and we had signed him to give our team added batting strength. But, to my utter amazement, Pete had only one arm. I found out later that he had lost his arm in a mining accident at the age of eight, and had had his arm amputated six inches below his right shoulder. The first game Pete played for us, we were playing Quebec City, and he started in center field. It was a thrill to see him catch the ball with his left hand and tuck his glove under his right stub and rifle the ball into the infield. He never lost any motion and he could run like a deer. The first time Pete had to bat, he slowly walked from the dugout to the batting rack to select a bat. Everyone in the dugout stood to watch as he selected a 42 ounce Jimmy Foxx bat, one of the heaviest bats being used in baseball today. As I looked through the stands, all eyes were riveted on this one-armed ball player. As he stood in the batter's box, with his bat resting on his left shoulder, a feeling of tenseness fell over the ball park. Pete watched the first pitch streak by for strike one, and the second for strike two. I wondered if he would be able to get that huge bat around with one arm. I also wondered if this could be a publicity stunt; or could he play organized ball. I got my answer on the next pitch, for he slashed a line drive to right field for a two-base hit. I shall never forget the ovation that Pete received. I saw 10,000 Canadians rise to show their respect for a one-armed ball player.

I was to learn later that Pete Gray was a rugged soul — he never thought of being handicapped, he never felt he was at a disadvantage. He gave baseball all he had, and it was good enough to get to the major leagues. Yes, Pete Gray played with the St. Louis Browns in the American League.

Pete Gray was all man and he knew he had the supreme power to seize fate by the throat and dictate his terms. He knew that destiny was not a matter of chance — but a matter of choice.

Pete was small in stature but big in heart, for courage makes one big; there is no place for crawling, worrying, cringing and whimpering for these are the tentacles of smallness and timidity. Yesterday's heartaches, fading hopes, sorrows and unfulfilled desires are suppressed by the person who is going forward. The lives of some of the greatest men are heroic by the fact that their handicaps became stimuli to have them accomplish even greater things and live greater lives. Courage coupled with mediocre ability many times has won over the much better equipped adversary. It is courage and courage alone that kept some persons striving for victory when the odds seemed long against them.

It was courage that drove Lou Burdette on to win three games in the 1957 World Series against the New York Yankees. It was sheer courage that spurred Franklin D. Roosevelt on to the presidency of the United States, even though he was handicapped with infantile paralysis. Floyd Collins, who was trapped in a cave in Kentucky, lived seven days before he died from exposure. Doctors said courage alone kept him living as long as he did.

Courage comes in many different packages, in various sizes, shapes and forms, but all call for extra effort by the person being asked to deliver.

Last Saturday while shopping at Sears and Roebuck I saw courage being demonstrated by a little girl eleven years old. We will call her Marie. Marie was dressed in yellow "bermudas" as most children are at that age, but Marie had only one leg. So Marie had decided she would be as other girls and wear "mudas." Of course, her artificial leg showed and most everyone stopped and stared at little Marie, whose courage was shining like a star in the sky. But little Marie just moved along, fully aware of the eyes that shadowed her, wearing what she wanted to. I, too, turned and stared, but as I did I shot a little prayer for Marie. A prayer that thanked the Lord for giving Marie courage to be as other girls are — God Bless You, Marie.

Walt Disney applied for a job at the Kansas City Star as an artist. They told him to forget his ambition because he lacked talent. Then he originated "Oswald the Rabbit." That, too, failed. Then, with everyone telling him to quit and get a job, he came up with "Mickey Mouse." Are you beginning to see the picture?

Robert Ripley was fired from his first job at a newspaper office. He was told he didn't have originality. Zane Grey didn't sell a story for six years.

Harriet Beecher Stowe wrote *Uncle Tom's Cabin* on sheets of butcher's paper while she was cooking dinner for her family.

How do you know what you can or can't do? What makes you think you can't write a book? Have you ever tried to write a lyric? Have you ever tried to improve on that idea you have been thinking about?

There is greatness in everyone; it's right in front of you. It's in the scheme, plan, idea, notion, dream or fancy that is on the threshold of becoming a reality. All you have to do is create a burning desire for the achievement of it.

In Bingham, Massachusetts, a man was out of work. To pass his time, he would whittle toys from shingles. The children fought for his toys. So he whittled more doll toys.

Then one day he put a few in a shoe store — today he's worth $100,000,000.

Another man was out of work, and Christmas was just thirty days away. He decided he would make Christmas toys for his children. He started by cutting blocks of wood, and he would name the blocks, hotels, railroads, utilities, etc. Then he made a cardboard chart where one could place these utilities, hotels, railroads, etc. — have you heard of "Monopoly?"

There was a mouse who was afraid of the cat. So the mouse went to a magician and begged him to turn him into a cat. This the magician did. Then a dog came along and the cat ran to the magician once more and begged to become a dog. This the magician did. After he became a dog, he realized he was no match for the leopard. So, once more he begged the magician, to become a leopard. Again, the magician granted him his wish and he pranced around until he met the lion. Again he went to the magician, but the magician refused. The magician said, "You have the heart of a mouse. I cannot change that, so no matter what you appear to be, you are still a mouse at heart. So I'm returning you to what you originally were: a mouse. You cannot become anything greater than the heart you have."

It's interesting to read about the six year old boy who was sent home from school because the teacher said he was stupid. His mother said, "He's not stupid. I'll teach him myself." The boy's name was Thomas Edison!

History tells us that Napoleon cheated at cards; that Henry VIII was a gambling addict and spent a great deal of his time rolling dice; that Nebuchadnezzar went into the fields and ate grass with the cows; that Sir Walter Scott had a fear of ghosts; and that Ben Franklin had a plate of bread and cheese by his side while studying. His reason was "to repair mental waste." All these men were famous and, despite their unusual activities, they made their mark.

Too many people are afraid of what people will think of them, when the important thing is what they think of themselves. The people who criticize and analyze you can't have much going on in their "thinking machine" or they would be too busy to notice your peculiarities.

It's hard for me to believe that we were put on this earth with equal talents. I listen to Frank Sinatra, Sammy Davis, Dinah Shore, and many other talented singers and I envy them. With their fame, fortune, and living style, it must be wonderful. (I don't agree with everything they do).

However, this I'm positive of: the Lord has blessed us with all the determination, desire, ambition, faith, and courage we'll ever need. All we have to do is recognize that we have it and use it. We have an infinite supply. There is also a belief that says "Use it or lose it."

What we must determine is what we want out of life — then go full speed ahead, using all the blessings that God has bestowed upon us.

My experience has been that too many people have a general idea of how successful they would like to be, but beyond that, things are vague. They merely go along drifting, like a cork on a river, drifting downward.

Invariably, as the years drift by they have a more distorted and morbid outlook on life. They feel sorry for themselves.

A young man, who had decided early in life that everyone and everything was against him, decided to commit suicide. His explanation to himself was that the world was against him, his employer was against him, he never got a break, and the girls didn't care for him. All in all he thought he'd make everyone happy and take his life.

Early the next morning he climbed up on a hugh bridge that spanned a river. He was just about to jump and end it all when he decided he'd better "right himself with the Lord" before he died.

He knelt to pray, looking up to the heavens as he did. "Oh Lord," he said — about that time a bird flew over his head, dropping something, as birds do. This something landed on the young fellow's forehead.

The young fellow reached up and with his handkerchief wiped it off. As he did, he said, "You see what I mean, Lord — for everyone else he sings."

THINKING

Archimedes was a great mathematician and inventor, of ancient Greece. His friend, the King, was worried that the goldsmith who made his gold crown had not used all the gold he had given him and had substituted a base metal.

The King wanted Archimedes to check the purity of the crown, but without damaging it in any way.

One day when Archimedes was taking a bath and relaxing, the answer came to him. Archimedes was jubilant that he had found the way to check the purity of the crown. The thought had occurred to him to take three identical vessels, each containing an equal amount of water, and put the crown in the first jar, the amount of gold the King had given him in the second, and an equal volume of silver in the third and then note the difference in the amount of over-flow of water from each.

Archimedes was a thinker and became one of the most respected thinkers in the history of Greece.

Another fellow who did a bit of thinking was the man who ran into the barber shop one Saturday morning and said to the barber at the head chair, "How many ahead of me?" "Two haircuts," responded the barber. The man rushed out, but didn't come back. The next Saturday, when the fellow dashed in with his inquiry, the barber said, "Three ahead of you, sir," . . . but the fellow was gone. "Follow that man and find out who he is," the barber instructed the shine boy. This is the third Saturday he has run in here, asked how many ahead of him, then, has run out and not come back." A few minutes later the shine boy returned. "Boss," he said, "Ah doan know who dat fella is, but ah sho' know where he went!" "Where?" asked the barber. "To yoah house, suh!"

There was a porter on the New York Central railroad who was serving drinks to two gentlemen in the club car. It was a

Monday night and business was brisk. As one of the gentlemen paid the porter he noticed a huge scar on the porter's face. He said, "Millard, where did you get that scar?" "Well, boss," replied the porter, "I was talking when I should have been listening and thinking."

Senator Carter Glass said of a talkative colleague, "When he gets started his tongue is like a race horse; it runs faster, the less weight it carries."

There is an old cliché that says, "An empty cart rattles the loudest."

If you say women are gabbier than men, you are not just talking through your hat, according to a researcher who has been counting their words.

The average businessman speaks 11,580 words a day, but his wife speaks 12,620. A waitress spoke 12,900 words a day; a policeman 10,660; a soldier 7,800; a priest 3,420; and a monk 860 words.

There have been many jokes written about women talking. Of course, the important thing is what they say.

I heard some women talking the other day about a new organization. It's an organization where women say they want to pay their own way on dates; they also say they don't want expensive presents on their birthdays; and they say they don't want men to give them their seats on buses. This organization is called Women's Fib.

There is an art in silence and there is an eloquence in it, too. But listening has become a lost art. A good listener is hard to find.

Barbers are perhaps the most well known listeners. This story illustrates. The barber asked, "Are you taking a vacation this year?" The man in the chair said, "Yes, in fact my wife and I are flying to Rome tomorrow for a couple of weeks." Barber: "How are you going?" Customer: "By United." Barber: "Don't go by United. The service is poor, the food is lousy, the stewardesses are ugly and it'll be rough all the way. Where are you staying in Rome?" Customer: "At the Hilton." Barber: "Don't stay there — you won't like it. The food is no good, the beds are hard and nobody will pay attention to you. You can find a better place to stay than that. What are you going to do in Rome?" Customer: "We thought we would try to get an audience with the Pope." Barber: "Take my advice, don't waste your time; you'll never get near him. There'll be ten thousand Italians milling around the square smelling like garlic. You'll wish you had never gone near the place." The fellow paid his bill and walked out. Three weeks later, he was back. Barber: "Did you go to Italy?" Customer: "Yep." Barber: "How did you go?" Customer: "We went by United. It was a wonderful trip, smooth sailing all the way. The food was excellent, the service great and the stewardesses were outstanding. Couldn't have been better." Barber: "Where did you stay?" Customer: "At the Hilton. It's a beautiful place, the food was terrific, the beds were soft and the accommodations were wonderful!" Barber: "Did you see the Pope?" Customer: "Yes, we did. We had a good half hour with him. There were only about a half dozen people and we didn't have to wait more than five minutes. It was the highlight of the trip." Barber: "Well, what did he say?" Customer: "As I knelt at his feet to receive his blessing, he looked at me and said, 'For Pete's sake, man! Where did you get that miserable haircut?'."

All of us would profit by uttering this prayer every morning: "Oh Lord, help me to keep my big mouth shut until I know what I'm talking about . . . Amen."

Many years ago a farmer in Pennsylvania decided to sell his farm and go to Canada to get coal oil for his cousin. Before he left he studied all about it. Then he sold his farm for $833.00 and went to Canada.

The new owner went out to a stream one day that had several planks across it. He noticed the cows would not drink the water. He called in the State geologists and they found that the water had a black filmy substance on it. They also found that this substance was a derivative of coal oil. This find was worth $100,000,000.

The man had studied all about coal oil, yet he failed to recognize the assets in his own backyard.

Was this poor judgment? Yes. He failed to take inventory of what he had. Too many of us do the same thing. All this farmer had to do was look. Instead, he was dreaming of riches in someone else's backyard.

If you are to be a more knowledgeable person and enjoy a more successful life, now is the time — not tomorrow, not the next year, but right now. The best preparation for a better "you" next year and the years after, is to look around you now and evaluate what you have. All the dreaming of a richer, fuller, more successful life is of little importance unless we make each day count — this very day you're living. If you'll follow this formula, you will find that each day you live will be the most successful, happiest day — for it is in the little pieces of accomplishments along the way that make for a successful, happy life.

A PIECE OF IRON

Did you ever think what would happen to a plain piece of iron worth five dollars? Made into horseshoes it would be worth $10. If it were made into needles, it would be worth $3,000, and if it were turned into main springs for watches, it would be worth $150,000. The value is determined by what you do with the material. The same is true of another material — you!

The things that happen to you just don't happen — they are caused. Whether it's fame, riches, or accomplishments that you want in life, there is a price you must pay.

They say the finest fruit is the farthest out on the limb. What I'm saying is that part of the price you must pay for success is to be willing to gamble. You must try to get to the fruit farthest out on the limb.

We could go on talking about the price for success; there are many facets that play an important role. But nothing worthwhile is for sure. There is always the element of risk.

So, if you are on the brink of a decision, evaluate first, then act. Too many people just wait. Success is not obtained by waiting. Success has a price — pay the price by making a decision. For if you wait, you have made a decision — for no decision is a decision in itself.

The successful businessman must not only be willing to gamble, but he must know what he's doing. He should be like Lady Godiva. She put all she had on a horse. She didn't win, but she sure showed.

In athletics the keynote is practice. I've seen golfers practice a nine iron shot for an hour. That's the price you pay to be a good golfer — practice.

Ben Hogan, one of the greatest golfers that ever lived, was only five-feet seven and weighed one-hundred fifty-five pounds. He knew that physically he could not compete with

Sam Snead, Julius Boros, Byron Nelson and so many of the other fine golfers of his day. But this he did know: he would out-practice them. The stories tell us that his hands would bleed from practicing so much.

To emphasize this to people going in sales, or any phase of business, has been a cardinal principle of mine — go over the fundamentals, the "demo," the sales pitch, description of a product, or go over the history of the individual or the company which you want to sell. Then I tell them I don't want them to be like one fellow. This man had a set routine, he got up at a certain hour and he ate at a certain hour. Every night before he went to bed he knelt down and said his prayers the same way every night. As years passed by he started to change. First of all, he had the Lord's Prayer printed on a large piece of cardboard that he hung over his bed. Then every night as he'd get ready to say his prayers, he'd stand by his bed, point to the Lord's Prayer on the wall and say, "Lord, dems my sentiments."

There are people today who are always looking for the short cut, the easiest way out or path of least resistance. We should call these people the "pausers" because they are usually pausing, doing just enough so they won't be fired. They, too, have their "pause that refreshes." The trouble is the pauses could last for hours.

We are all going to have our disappointments and we should give thanks for them. For without them we could not appreciate accomplishments. Today success is easy because most people take the road of least resistance — they have reached their level of being satisfied. They have forgotten about determination; their goals were packed away long ago. In short, they are lazy — they have resigned themselves to their little pigeon-holes where they can sit and watch the other guy go up the ladder of success.

The winner steps up the stairs. A loser stares up the steps.

For the person who has ambition, who becomes excited in what he's doing and is willing to constantly improve his abilities, success is a surety. You need not worry about the other 75% — they discourage easily and are content with their pigeon-holes. Intelligence and determination puts you in the upper 25%. Persistence and enthusiasm put you in the upper 10%. Success is yours if you are willing to get excited about it.

It seems that a country church caught on fire and all the town folks came to help or watch. After all, the church doesn't burn down everyday! At this fire was "Heathen Charlie." Someone said, "Charlie, this is the first time I've seen you at church." "Yes," said Charlie, and it's the first time there's been any fire in it." — I like "fire" in people: the fire of enthusiasm, the fire of determination, and the burning desire of accomplishment.

Swift says, "It is in men as in soils, sometimes a vein of gold you know not, can be uncovered, during the time you waste, by digging within yourself." You are not safe if you are doing today what you did yesterday. If you are thinking today as you thought yesterday, your motor is running down. For life is growing and anticipating; death is idling and quitting. To be alive in this world of accomplishments is to dream, to have desires, to be willing to take a chance and have that positive feeling of anticipating success.

Roger Williams, the famous pianist, says, "If you want fame and fortune you have to pay for them. . . . When I'm home I practice the piano eight to ten hours a day. When I'm on the road, I practice two to three hours per day. Discipline is the key to my success. No matter how tired I am I practice." Roger Williams' hit album *Autumn Leaves* sold 15 million records. He said his love for music and his passion for self-discipline began when he was eleven years old and his parents took him to hear Ignace Paderewski. After hearing Paderewski he was determined to be a great pianist. "My goal," he said, "was to be as good as the great Paderewski." He knew it would take long years of hard work on this journey to be great. Roger Williams traveled this journey to become great. He overcame heartaches and disappointments and continued on. Now that he has arrived, he is planning for even a better future in his new journey.

Would you like to take a journey to success? Let's call this a journey *of* success, not *to* success. All along the way you will appreciate all the good things that happen to you as success. Whatever you want, be it money, friends, new position, all can be yours if you plan your trip. All along you are going to see your dreams and hopes unfold as you go forward. You are going to see a change. You will become the person you want to be. Your thinking will become positive, with a feeling of expecting good things to happen. You are successful because you have started on your journey. Success is not a destination, but a journey.

THE OTHER GUY

We sometimes envy the other guy
Who seems to do things right,
And wonder why the breaks don't come
Though we try with all our might.

You think the other guy is lucky,
That breaks keep drifting his way.
But, if you'd look a little deeper,
He's had his discouraging day.

He knows what it means to struggle,
To really try with all his heart.
And this other guy has wondered
If it was right for him to start.

On the outside it looked so easy.
On the inside he had to try.
With work, faith, and desire
You, too, can be the other guy.

The other guy didn't just become the other guy.

—Roy Pinyoun

OPEN THE DOOR

Opportunity is a great deal like the new girl who moves into the neighborhood. She's cute, has the necessary accessories, has a pleasing smile and wonderful personality. In fact, she's the nicest thing that's happened to the neighborhood in some time. You entertain the thought of dating her, but "old man doubt" steps in and you rationalize your doubt by saying "She wouldn't date me." While you're evaluating yourself, someone else steps in and, wham, she dates him. They eventually go steady and a few years later they get married. What about you? You will always wonder what would have happened had you taken advantage of the opportunity.

Bernard Baruch, one of the wisest, wealthiest statesman this country has ever known, said that timing is the most important ingredient to success. Knowing how to recognize opportunity and to take advantage of it. To act, to say, "this is my opportunity, I shall act *now*."

Never forget that what you think about yourself is precisely what other people think of you — for others' attitudes reflect themselves in our outlook. If others like us, we return the admiration.

Dr. Louis Bisch, one of the nation's leading psychiatrists, wrote, "Cultivate a little of the don't-care habit; don't worry about what other people think. This will endear you to others and make you liked and loved all the more."

The door of opportunity can be opened by decision and determination, but only by *your* decision and your determination.

I'm reminded of the story of the young man in the bus station. He had to go to the washroom, but had no money. So he asked an elderly gentleman if he would loan him a dime. The gentleman did, and the young man hurried to the washroom. As he was about to deposit his dime in the door slot, someone opened the door. The young man put the dime back in his pocket and proceeded in.

Later that day, the young man used his only dime to play the slot machine. Fortune was good to him for he hit the jackpot and won $43.00. The young man was overwhelmed by his good fortune and decided he would try his luck at the race track. Again fortune smiled for he won the "daily double" and now had $8750.00.

As the years went by this young man parlayed his track winnings with good investments and accumulated a fortune.

At a businessmen's luncheon one day, he related his story of how it all happened from the day in the bus station. One of his business acquaintances said "I'll bet you'd like to meet the gentleman who gave you that dime." "No," he replied, "I'd like to meet the man that opened the door."

NOTHING TO UNLOAD

It took me a long time to learn this lesson — be prepared. Sometime, somewhere you will be asked to come forward and say a few words. If you have something to say, say it and sit down. Whatever you say, keep it brief — you were not planned for a big part of the program. I can emphasize this best by quoting Franklin D. Roosevelt. He said, "Be sincere, be brief, be seated."

What should you do if you can't find something appropriate to say? Believe me, this will happen if you are in the "people business" long enough.

When this happens, you walk slowly and confidently to the podium, you smile at everyone and shake hands with the person who asked you to say a few words.

With an air of confidence you say:

A farmer was driving home in a truck loaded with potatoes. It was a rainy day and the dirt road had become quite muddy. As the farmer started up a steep hill the tailgate opened and the potatoes rolled out, unknown to him. A little farther up the hill his truck got stuck in the mud. He thought to himself, "I'll just have to lessen the load by removing the potatoes." The farmer got out of the truck and, to his surprise, all his potatoes had rolled out.

"Well friends, I feel a great deal like the farmer, stuck without anything to unload. Thank you very much."

Then sit down!

CHILDREN

The child lives for today. As we grow older, we forget that today is really the only important day of our lives.

There are those who dwell in the past, involved with the family tree and who their illustrious grandparents were, but no one really cares.

When I first moved to Raleigh, one of my neighbors spent an evening telling me how his grandfather would ride a $26,000 horse with a beautiful silver buckle saddle, over his plantation. I remember that evening well. I had wished the horse had stepped on his tongue.

Then we have the "future waiters." They scrimp and save and plan for a day that's just "round the corner;" they never get there. Finally the doc says, "Better slow up — the old ticker. You've been working too hard."

Can you picture a youngster doing that? His secret of living is playing each hour to the fullest. He'll play until the last flicker of sunlight drops beyond the horizon.

The carefree years slip by so fast; yesterday they were children playing with marbles, tomorrow they are talking of college, and before you know it, they're in their own apartment. My hat's off to the children and for what they stand for — freshness, purity, love, sincerity, honesty and innocence. If only we were smart enough to learn from them.

Last Halloween I was home alone. About nine o'clock someone rang our doorbell. As I opened it I saw a beautiful little girl about six years old. She had long blonde hair spread across her shoulders; blue eyes that seemed to glitter as she said, "Trick or Treat." I was awe-struck by her poise, her cute mouth, that long white dress that made her look like a precious little princess. My first impression was to pick her up and hold her, for she was the picture of "child loveliness." Until now, we had been giving the children Tootsie

Rolls, but for this little lady that wasn't good enough. I went to the kitchen and picked out a large California orange. I held the orange up and a big smile crept across her face. She opened up her bag and I dropped the orange in it. She looked at me, looked in her bag — she didn't say a word. I thought she was surprised at getting such a huge orange. She looked in the bag again, then looked up at me and said, "Mister, you've broken all my damn cookies."

Yes, children can be many things; perhaps unpredictable should head the list. To elaborate further on this, I'd like to relate this story.

A mother was putting her five year old son to bed. As she tucked him in, she said, "Shh, the sandman is coming." The little boy looked up and said. "Give me a quarter and I won't tell daddy." Can you imagine that? It used to be a dime!

Family life can be the source of the greatest happiness. This happiness is pure and costs so little and cannot be bought. It is the foundation of tomorrow for America. For America's hope, growth, development and freedom will be shouldered by these youngsters. Their abilities will reflect our part in their lives.

Of course some families are over-burdened with too many children. I'm reminded of the Catholic lady who wrote to her priest. She asked permission to use some means of birth control. Some time later her permission was denied. One day she was shopping with six of her ten children, when she saw the priest. The priest said, "Mrs. Angelo, it's so nice to see you and what a lovely family you have." Mrs. Angelo was exhausted and the thought of going home and cooking for her family did not elevate her spirits. Finally, she said to the priest, "Father Donahue, can I ask you a personal question?" "Of course," replied the priest. Mrs. Angelo said, in broken English, "How come you make-a da rules and you no play-a da game?"

WHAT DO YOU SEE?

A king had three sons and was undecided as to which one would rule the kingdom. So he told them to mount their horses and follow him. As they rode through the woods, the King spotted a vulture sitting on a limb of a tree. The King told his first son to get off his horse and take aim at the vulture.

Before he shot the arrow the King said, "First, tell me what you see."

The son said, "I see the green grass, the trees, the blue sky."

"That's enough," said the King, "Get back on your horse."

The King told his second son to get off his horse and prepare to shoot the vulture.

"But first, what do you see?" asked the King.

The second son said that he, too, saw the clear blue sky, the trees, etc.

The King said, "Get back on your horse."

Now it was the third son's time. He jumped off his horse and prepared to shoot his arrow.

Before he fired, he said, "I see the point where the wings join the body," and he let his arrow fly. The arrow was true on its mark and hit the vulture in that exact point. This son would be the next king.

There is a moral to this story. The man who shoots for everything and nothing in particular will probably hit nothing.

But the man who sets his sights on one goal will attain it.

Are you going to hit your target? Do you have your aim on the target? The man with a goal who will allow nothing to distract his view will hit his target, will reach his goal.

What do you see? Do you see a new home, a car, furniture,

or a college education for your children? Set your sights on your goal and keep it implanted in your mind, never forgetting what the wise old King asked, "What do you see?"

Every morning when you wash your face and brush your teeth, you are looking at the most important person in the world. Know that, and be satisfied in what you see. You have powers within you that are untapped. You can do things you never thought you could do. There are no limits to what you can do, if you see yourself doing it. Have big goals and big dreams, for you never get bigger than the goals you set.

I want you to think as the little old lady did as she was in the grips of a big, swarthy, ugly thug. The little old lady handed over her money and said, "You ought to be ashamed of yourself, stealing from a helpless old lady. You should be robbing a bank."

It's discouraging to see unfulfilled, unrealized ambitions, and the door of opportunity closed for lack of use, all because we didn't push for our goal.

An old philosopher once said, "When you are through preparing yourself for the future, you are really through. The future is waiting for the man who is prepared and willing to pursue it."

There was a race horse that won every race — in fact, the other horses refused to run against this horse. The owner was so proud that he retired the horse and painted these words on the side of his huge barn, "This is the fastest horse this world has ever known." One year later he decided to race his horse again. The horse had not kept pace with the future, he had not trained. In his first race the horse finished last. The owner was humiliated and disgusted, and he once again retired his horse to the pasture. He repainted his barn with these words: "This is the fastest world this horse has ever seen."

Men who have accomplished great things in life have discovered that it was easy because the average man only does what he has to do. He is lazy and tries to get by with the least possible effort. My "average man" thinks of only "what do I get paid and when do I get off?"

Now and then an unusual man comes along who is not content with mediocrity. This man finds life interesting and challenging. His days are filled with ideas, plans and dreams of the future. He is constantly thinking, plotting and planning for better things and better days. If you've never thought about a goal, think now. Here's what you do! Write down what you want!

(a) Visualize it happening.

(b) Look at your goal first thing in the morning and at bed time.

(c) Eliminate all fears.

(d) Remember! It's easier to think negatively—that's why 95% of the people do it.

Emerson said, "You reap what you sow!" What are you sowing? You sow good seeds and you'll get good results for yourself and others. The secret to being successful is to contribute something. You don't make money; they make money in the mint. You only earn money when you're successful and contributing to the benefit of others. No man can really be rich until he shares his ideas, plans, thoughts and future.

We must constantly remember, as we venture, that there will be those who can tell us many reasons why something won't work. This is that 95% negative influence. What we must remember is that we only need one reason why it will.

BE A STARTER

Someone said, "it couldn't be done,"
But I didn't believe them at all.
I was convinced it would be so
If I didn't get on the ball.

A negative person will tell you
All the reasons it can't be done,
That the battle of life is unfair
And it's not meant for everyone.

Then I think of Beethoven and Edison,
Steinmetz, and Ford as a few,
And a "loser" probably told them
Just as he's telling you.

Be sincere in what you believe,
Then do it with all your heart.
For a person will never succeed
If he never decides to start.

—Roy Pinyoun

J. Paul Getty, who is one of the wealthiest men in the world, was asked, "How did you become so wealthy?"

His reply, "I tried harder."

To J. Paul Getty it was a personal thing, his goal was to become very wealthy.

We all need a goal, something that makes us want to get up in the morning and stay up late at night; something that keeps spurring us on, and provides that confident feeling that we'll reach it, because we're trying harder.

They say the crowd loves a winner, respects a loser, but

hates a quitter. This, again, is your decision. You must decide.

It's like the girl caught in a severe wind and hail storm — should she hold her umbrella or her skirt? She had to make the decision.

What you receive in life will be in direct proportion to what you put out — the effort you exert. If your efforts are feeble, your results will be feeble.

It's like the couple who was trying to make ends meet with a meager salary. No matter how they tried, they just didn't have money enough to go around. The wife, who was busy changing the baby's diaper, said, "Maybe I should get a job."

The husband walked over, picked up the baby and said, "We're in bad shape — this is the only thing that's paid for and it leaks."

In a mid-western state, where farming is the predominant way of living, there was a severe drought. The drought had lasted so long that should the farmers not get rain soon their crops would be a total loss.

The church in this particular community had a new young pastor who decided he would do something about it. He announced on the following Sunday that there would be an outdoor prayer meeting for everyone on Monday. He felt with everyone there, praying for rain, that the Lord would oblige. The congregation all agreed and enthusiastically looked forward to Monday night.

As the people gathered on Monday night, both the young and old, there was one little girl of nine who brought an umbrella. She was the only one who had faith.

It has always amazed me how little children have faith and honestly believe that things can become what you believe. Perhaps it's innocence, but we could use a little of their faith.

A teacher told her class of first graders to get a piece of paper and they could draw anything they wanted. Then the teacher walked around asking the children what they were drawing. The children would reply and the teacher would smile and nod her head. The teacher paused, and with a look of bewilderment she said, "Mary, what are you drawing?"

Mary said, "I'm drawing a picture of God."

The teacher, being very careful in replying, said, "But, Mary, we don't know what God looks like."

Mary looked up with her blue eyes full of confidence and said, "We do now."

You must keep moving toward your goal. Don't hesitate or stop for fear of making an error. You can always correct your error if you are moving. It's like riding a bicycle, you can correct your direction while moving, but if you stop you become shaky and fall.

Once you have decided where you are, who you are and where you want to go, you are successful. So start now, without hesitation or fear, for it is doing that that gives you power to be successful and to reach your goal.

Above all, try with all your might. Let every fiber in your body feel the effort as you try harder. The secret of trying harder is self motivation. Tell yourself constantly that this is your big opportunity and you'll not let it pass you by.

I want you to be like the race horse that was winning every race. Now when a horse wins every race, other jockeys begin to wonder if the jockey is giving the horse drugs. That's exactly what happened, so the other jockeys decided they would hide in the stable and see what the jockey was doing to the horse. Finally the winning jockey walked over to his horse and whispered in his ear.

"Roses are red,
Violets are blue.
Horses that lose
Are turned into glue."

We have a goal; we're going to try harder. Now we must have faith. Faith in knowing we are going to get from life what we're trying for. Expect victory, and we'll get victory.

"Therefore I say unto you, what things ye desire, when ye pray believe that ye receive them and ye shall have them," said the Master.

TIME

Life is a game of chess and your opponent is a persistent one; he is not the greatest, he is not the fastest, but like the turtle he keeps crawling along. If you stagger a little, if you pause and show signs of doubt, he will pass you by. If he passes you, the game is over. You have lost forever. Do you know who your opponent is? . . . *Time*.

Time is the one thing that can never be regained. You may lose and regain wealth; you may lose and regain a friend; and opportunity could strike again; but the time you lose through idleness can never be recaptured. Most careers are synonymous with what we do with our time.

It has been said that money and time are the heaviest burdens of life. The unhappy person is the one who has so much of each that he doesn't know how to use it.

Time is important because we don't know how much we have. So the secret is to plan as if you'll live forever — and live as if this were your last day.

The next time you are washing your face, look up and ask the person in the mirror, "What is the most important thing for you to do?" What do you suppose the answer would be? Perhaps you might say "make money," or "buy a new suit," "work in the yard," "play golf," "take a nap," "read a book," or "make out reports." I'm sure we could stand there and list a multitude of things we could or should do.

Now, let's suppose we only had one day to live. What would you do? Would you try to pack everything possible in those last twenty-four hours? In other words, would you *live* those twenty-four hours? You would look around you and see people not taking advantage of all the wonderful things, of not living each day to the fullest.

I'm sure this farmer wasn't too worried about living each day to the fullest. It's where you place your values.

A man from the North was visiting Georgia and met a farmer with a drove of hogs. The Northerner said, "Where are you taking those hogs?" "To the woods, so they can eat acorns," said the farmer. "Up North we keep them in a pen and feed them corn." "What for?" asked the farmer. "Why, it saves time," replied the Northerner. The farmer said, "What's time to a hog?"

Napoleon Hill says the secret of a full life is to eat sparingly, work enthusiastically, save time for playing everyday, and love generously.

What we do with our time is a personal matter. We should not be like the teacher who was rebuked by one of his students. This teacher saw one of his students fishing and said, "Young man, you should be tending your lessons. Your time must not be very valuable. I've been watching you and you haven't had a bite in two hours." "Well, 'teach'," said the young boy, "I consider my time too valuable to waste two hours of it watching another guy fishing when he ain't catching anything."

Time has a way of showing what we are by our habits. These habits tell the story of what we've been, a thoroughbred or an also-ran. By selecting our habits we determine how we'll run in the race of life.

Have you ever seen a thoroughbred? There is something about the way he holds himself that shows his breeding and training. He holds his head high; he walks with a determined, rhythmical gait, and has a sleek, confident appearance. That's a real thoroughbred!

An African tribe has a unique custom. When anyone makes a speech they must stand on one leg. When the other leg touches the floor, the speech is automatically over.

Time is a regulated income and, as any income, the secret is to live within our daily allotment. So take time to think, work, play, read, laugh, give and pray — it's a God-given privilege.

"Oh God, give me the wisdom to recognize that the time I have is limited and grant me the courage and desire to use it wisely."

THE DIFFERENCE

Everyone walking down the street
Is a little bit different than me.
With millions of people all over the world
And never a pair you'll see.

Outwardly some resemble one another,
But look inside and you'll find
Their difference shows up in their thinking—
It's all in the state of mind.

Some see life through rose-colored glasses,
With everything dancing and gay.
Others see fate with negative thoughts,
And troubles always coming their way.

But the Master has been most generous
I'm happy in all I can see.
I'm grateful that I can control
The thoughts that come out of me.

Thoughts have been the way of
every path you've taken.

Roy Pinyoun

THE PIECE OF SUGAR

Bernard Baruch, a German Jew, immigrated to this country at an early age. As the ship was sailing into the harbor, Baruch saw the Statue of Liberty for the first time. His eyes became as large as saucers as excitement and anticipation spread across his face. His father, being an intelligent man, looked at his excited son and said, "Son, I want to caution you that you are going to have problems here, just as you had in Germany. Your playmates will make fun of you because you're a foreigner and because you speak broken English. They may even fight you."

Baruch, later in life, said the greatest piece of advice he ever received was when his father said, "Son, it isn't important where you've come from or what you've done; the important thing is where you're going and what you are going to do."

Baruch was a quiet, courteous, distinguished gentleman who calmly and wisely advised six presidents. Bernard Baruch said, "No one can humiliate me, I won't let them." He, at age thirty-three was worth thirty-three million dollars. Not letting anyone humiliate him reminds me of this story.

It was the week of the State Fair. Elmer and Dora were enjoying all the shows when they were confronted with a cage that had a fierce man-eating tiger in it. Everyone was waiting for the show to start, so Elmer and Dora decided they'd wait too. About this time a cute little lady entered the cage and put the fierce tiger through such a series of stunts that the crowd gasped. Dora was so thrilled and excited that she turned to Elmer and said, "Isn't she wonderful, isn't she brave?" Elmer showed absolutely no emotion.

As the finale, this pert little trainer put a piece of sugar in her mouth and the tiger came and bit it out of her mouth. Dora was shouting and clapping, she was so beside herself, she turned to Elmer and said, "Wasn't she wonderful?" "I didn't see anything so wonderful," said Elmer. "Do you think you could do that?" asked Dora. "I could," replied Elmer. "I'd like to see you," she snapped back. "Just get the tiger and I'll show you," he said.

We cheat ourselves of the things we could accomplish and the things we could have because we are afraid; we don't have the "guts" — the ability to take it. This ability to take it, can be yours if you'll stand your ground when you want to run; if you'll force a smile, when you want to cry; if you'll have visions of a better tomorrow. For the sun will always shine through the clouds of despair.

It isn't the size of the man in the fight, it's the size of the fight in the man.

"The world will step aside for the man who is determined to progress." Each one of us has this decision to make — to progress or stand still. If you do not go forward, you will go backward. There is no standing still.

Know what you want in life and pursue it. Set your goals; short term goals, long term goals — and always with a forward thrust. Always make your time count.

There was a visitor at a mental hospital who saw an inmate pushing a wheelbarrow upside down. When he asked the inmate why, he replied, "You think I'm crazy, do you? I pushed the wheelbarrow right side up yesterday and they kept filling it with gravel."

It is common knowledge that many people today who have set goals go around pushing their wheelbarrows right side up; they are content to let others dump worthless jobs in their wheelbarrows, instead of constructively pursuing their goals.

As the years drift by, they alibi; they say "Lady Luck" did not have them in the right place at the right time. "Lady Luck" does not supply the right place — you make it.

It's like the fellow who said to his friend, "I've broken my nose in three places, what do you think of that?" The fellow replied, "If I were you I'd stay out of those places."

THE PELICANS

For years the shrimp boats have gathered shrimp off the Florida shores. They would leave St. Augustine, Florida, every morning and net for shrimp all day. As the boats headed for home the men would start deheading the shrimp. They would put the heads in bushel baskets, and as they reached the docks, they would throw the refuse overboard.

The pelicans followed this operation daily, patiently waiting for the shrimp boats to throw their refuse overboard. As soon as the refuse hit the water the pelicans would swarm down and gorge themselves. They were taking advantage of the free lunch, the something for nothing. This went on for years. Then the shrimp beds gave out and the shrimp boats had to go farther down the coast of Florida. As for the pelicans, they didn't know what happened and they went hungry. It's historically true that thousands died from starvation. The pelicans had gotten soft — they didn't know how to make it on their own. They didn't know that you can't always get things for nothing; that you receive in direct proportion to your effort. The something for nothing is sheer fantasy. There is a price tag on everything. The pelicans had lost the art of working for what they needed.

But remember, work for work's sake is folly. We should see that our work is getting us somewhere. We should take the road that leads us to our goals. Too many people just take the road, not caring where it goes — just so the road or job feeds and takes care of their necessities. This isn't living — it's existing! Some people are afraid to fail. If you don't succeed at first, try again and again and again — but keep trying.

Columbus tried for 17 years to get someone to finance his trip. Thomas Edison tried 1650 different materials before settling on carbon as the filament for the electric light bulb. When they finally opened Thomas Edison's desk after his death they found a card that said, "Whenever you're down in the mouth, remember Jonah — he came out all right."

Oscar Hammerstein II had five flop shows that lasted less than six weeks each. Then he hit *Oklahoma* which ran for 2250 performances and grossed 7 million dollars on an $183,000 investment.

What you should understand is that you are an individual. You are unique. You, as a personality, are not in competition with any other personality. You are not and never will become like any other person. You are not supposed to be like any other person, and no other person is supposed to be like you.

Inferiority and superiority are opposite sides of the same coin. The truth about you is this: you are not inferior — you are not superior — *you are simply you!*

Now the question! What are you going to do with you? Are you going to wait for Social Security, and in the interim get some state or federal aid? Are you going to be like those sturdy individuals that kept trying? Or have you decided to be like the pelicans and settle for the free handout?

Life isn't easy! Sometimes we all wish we were like the young man who went to work in a large factory. His starting salary was very meager and his job was as a laborer. However, he was determined to climb up the ladder. After thirty days he was in charge of the shipping department and his salary had tripled. Two months later he was in the office. In one year this ambitious young fellow was called into the president's office. The president said, "You are the new President of this company at $75,000 per year!" "Thank you," said the young man. "Haven't you anything else to say?" asked the president. "Yes," replied the young fellow, "Tell Mother I won't be home for dinner."

BE PREPARED

Clarence E. Birdseye, in 1924, borrowed on his life insurance policy, borrowed all the money he could from the banks and invested it all in the frozen food business. He lost all his money when the venture failed.

Now, most people would have quit, but not Clarence Birdseye. He was confident that there was a market in frozen foods. He started over again with $7.00 and part of a friend's ice plant.

Clarence Birdseye became a multi-millionaire because he had faith in what he believed. He pictured himself as being successful in the frozen food business.

The secret is to see yourself as you want to be, the way Clarence Birdseye did.

As Sir Buxton said, "The longer I live, the more I'm certain that the great difference between men, between the feeble and the powerful, between the great and the also-ran . . . is energy! That invincible determination of energy coupled with the right purpose."

A great man once said, "I would rather attempt to do something great and fail, than to do nothing and succeed."

Goals are what motivate us, but more important they keep us alive. Not having a goal is a life without a purpose. Therefore, it is essential that we know what we want out of life.

This goal-setting is a personal matter, it's a deep-seated dream, obsession or whatever, that is in direct communication with your subconscious mind at all times.

What people should understand is that if they do not follow their own thoughts, then they will follow the thoughts of the fellow who followed his. You then become a follower instead of a leader.

This reminds me of the soldier who received three letters from his girl in one week. Although he was going on furlough in three weeks, those letters motivated him. He packed his bag and headed for the main gate, running as fast as he could. The sentry yelled, "Halt!" The soldier kept running, calling, "My mother's in heaven, my father's in hell, my girl's in Chicago, and I'm going to be with one of them tonight!"

Have you ever thought seriously about the Boy Scouts? It's an organization that originated in England, the idea being brought to this country in 1912. At the present time there are approximately two and one half million boy scouts in this country. The Boy Scouts have continually grown since its inception in 1912. Why? There are many reasons. Perhaps their motto, "Be Prepared," sums it up. We can learn from their motto to be prepared both mentally and physically. The Scouts also emphasize learning by doing.

Abe Lincoln's thirst for knowledge was unbelievable. He literally begged and borrowed every book he could get. It was a constant goal for Abe to continually keep learning. Perhaps the best way to sum it up would be by repeating a remark he made when he was a young man. "I know my time will come and I shall be prepared."

Later in life, Abe Lincoln was asked, "What is the secret of success?" He replied, "There are many things necessary for success, and each are equally important. They are work, work and work!"

We can learn the value of patience, courage, faith, and desire for knowledge from Abe Lincoln, for he realized that there was no shortcut to success.

Dr. Harvey Cushman, a brain surgeon, could cut off the top of your head, make repairs and place it back again. In thirty years he has completed 2000 brain operations. In the beginning he would lose nine out of ten patients during the operation. Now, he saves nine out of ten in this serious operation. He paid the price of success by being persistent.

Burne-Jones, the painter, was asked by a lady, "How do

you make that free-hand circle so perfect?'' ''It's easy, madam,'' he replied, ''All you have to do is practice two hours a day for forty years.''

These men all had a goal and they kept it foremost in their minds. They pictured themselves as being successful; they were prepared and they were willing to pay the price.

To be prepared is so important!

I don't want you to be like the preacher in the jungle who met a lion face-to-face. The preacher had no gun, so he dropped to his knees and prayed. To his amazement the lion crouched beside him. The preacher turned to the lion and said, ''Moments ago I feared for my life, now you're praying beside me.''

''Shut up,'' said the lion, ''I'm saying grace.''

SILENCE

George Jessel tells of the time he was to deliver an address. It was a typical banquet where many people had to be introduced and many more recognized from the floor. Then there were awards to be presented. Besides, the master of ceremonies enjoyed hearing himself talk. After three hours it was time for George Jessel. The M.C. started by telling about Jessel's school days; then his debut in radio; then in TV; then elaborated on his demand as a speaker. Finally, he was finished, saying "It gives me a great deal of pleasure to introduce George Jessel, who will now give you his address." George Jessel stood up and said, "My address is 1510 Park Avenue, New York City, New York," and he sat down.

Most meetings and banquets are too long. It is important to remember that: "The mind cannot absorb anymore than the tail can endure."

I've always made it a point to ask my wife after a meeting, "Was it too long? — was it interesting?" Then I ask her, "Did I do a good job?" She always says, "Yes." She says that, not because I'm clever, but because she is.

I'm sure we all talk too much at times. I think we should be more like the little boy of six who had never said a word. The doctors were puzzled for the boy was completely normal, and the parents were worried. One morning the boy sat down for breakfast, and to the astonishment of all, he said, "This hot chocolate is not hot!" The parents were so jubilant that they were lost as what to say. Finally, the father said, "Son, why haven't you talked before now?" The son looked up and said, "Up until now everything has been all right."

KEEP KNOCKING

There was a gun company in Germany that suspended a ten-pound steel bar by a chain. Beside the steel bar they suspended a four-gram cork. They arranged it in such a way that the cork would bump into the steel bar. Of course nothing happened when the small cork kept bumping into that ten-pound steel bar. However, they had the little cork keep bumping, bumping for two hours, then four hours, and, as we'd suspect, nothing would happen. But wait a minute! After ten hours the steel bar moved a little; then it moved a little more as the little cork kept pounding away. In twenty-four hours that little four-gram cork was controlling the motion of a ten-pound steel bar. How? By persistence of effort!

Persistence of effort! This is the key to success in most everything — especially athletics.

Johnny Weissmuller, whom most people will remember as Tarzan in the movies, at one time held sixty-seven swimming records. He was supreme in world competition at any distance between fifty yards and a half mile. In his prime he was powerful, with a tremendous chest. He could swim through the water with such force that his back was above the water. From 1921 until he retired from competition in 1929 he was King of the Waters. Now, through knowledge and persistence of effort, *sixteen year old girls* are breaking his records today!

It's being persistent that gets results. Success will come as it did to the wealthy Indian who had a number of oil wells in Oklahoma. When he was asked how he became so successful and rich he replied, "It's easy. I just kept on digging holes."

As Charles Kettering, the inventor, said, "The achievement of your goal is assured the moment you commit yourself to it. The realization will require time. Let your imagination dream, your goals direct, your enthusiasm propel and your persistence will produce."

A survey was taken which discovered that 80% of sales were made after the fifth call. Forty-eight percent of the salesmen quit after the first call. Twenty-five percent quit after the second call. Twelve percent quit after the third call. Ten percent of the salesmen kept calling and made eighty percent of the sales. Persistence is the key; it provides momentum. You can have it! It's up to you.

Everything today is persistence; our learning, our advertising, our success in athletics. It's the reading, reading, reading; the showing, showing, showing; and the practice, practice, practice. It's the concentrated persistency of effort that produces success.

It's up to you — the decision rests on your shoulders. Will you pay the price of persistency? Will you never give up? Will you never deviate from your purpose? If so, success can be yours.

There was a young fellow who was in love when his company transferred him out of town for a year. Being an intelligent young man, he knew the value of being persistent. So that his girl wouldn't forget him, he mailed her a letter every day. At the end of the year she got married — she married the mailman, for he was persistent too. He delivered the mail everyday and developed a friendship that eventually resulted in marriage.

I tell you this story to remind you that there are others who will be persistent. There will be others who will knock on the door of success. But you remember what Henry Wadsworth Longfellow said, "Having persistency and confidence that you will succeed and having the courage to keep knocking on the door of success until someone opens it; believe me, if you knock long and hard enough, they will open it."

THE VOLCANO

When you first look at a mountain, it impresses you by its size; you marvel at how long it has been standing there and you imagine how difficult it must have been for the earlier settlers to cross. Then, as you look you become a little disappointed at its vastness, the coldness of its greyish appearance. You wonder if it is actually characteristic of our American tradition of action and accomplishment, of growth and spirit moving ahead.

When you first look at a volcano, it is rather awesome with its bubbling lava that means destruction if not controlled. The hotness of its contents; the lethal results in its unexpected eruption of molten lava that mean potential disaster. However, after watching the activity of the volcano, you notice how it "turns on," it becomes alive. It keeps shaking and moving, it becomes light and it glows — it's something special.

In retrospect I feel that this is the way the Almighty wanted us to be — alive, moving, glowing, being "turned on," constantly anticipating, always utilizing the same sort of energy that lies deeply imbedded in the volcano.

The next time you look at a mountain, admire its vastness, but don't become passive as the mountain. Instead, be alive, be moving, be doing, be "turned on" — and most of all, let that energy that lies deep within come racing to propel you to the great things in this life. It was this infinite supply of energy that made it possible for man to fly over those mountains.

Don't be a mountain. Be a volcano. End product — *energy!* People could be like a volcano — some are! It's just a question of using our energy.

So the next time you have a goal to reach, think of the volcano, think of the power that is released by the volcano.

You too, have an infinite supply of energy, you too can move, get "turned on" and release that abundance that you always have stored within. Remember, all the energy you have is not worth a hill of beans until you release it and be a volcano!

Robert Browning said, "Ah, but a man's reach should exceed his grasp, or what's heaven for."

The Lord has blessed us with an abundance of energy, but we must supply the direction. If our direction is somewhat hazy, then ask the Lord. Pray — don't be ashamed. "More things are wrought by prayer than the world knows."

When you are confronted with a problem, isolate yourself and meditate, thinking things out. Then seek the Lord. Don't ask him to be on your team; you ask to be on His.

Be like the little boy who was saying his prayers. He was almost finished when his mother said, "You're not praying loud enough because I can't hear you." The little boy looked up and said, "This is personal. I'm just talking to the Lord."

VITAL 5%

George Burton Hutchins used to ask this question of his advertising class at New York University: "How much of the total effort involved in preparing an ad does the public see? Only 5%, but it's the vital 5% — it's the 5% that sells."

The 95% you don't see is the research, testing, planning, writing, layout, and selling. These are as important to the merchandising as the vital 5%.

In our early years our mother and dad teach us right and wrong and prepare us for school. Then we spend the next twelve years getting an education. Many more go to college which could add as many as ten more years. Why? Because we are preparing ourselves for the vital 5%. The interview fails to show the years of preparation, but it is essentially the key to your employment.

It's like planting a garden. We cultivate the ground; we fertilize the soil; — we water, weed, prune. We determine what to plant, then we wait for the vital 5% when we harvest our crops.

We are like the billboard and the garden. Every step along the way is necessary and important in preparation for the day when the public sees the billboard, the farmer reaps his harvest, and you have your interview. How the billboard is shown to the public, how good the harvest is, and how well you perform when interviewed, is all the vital 5%. The vital 5%, when you walk into the office, is of immediate importance because you never get a second opportunity to make a "first" impression. Another man was ready for the vital 5%!

I have a friend who inherited a great amount of money. He had always liked the races, so he bought a horse he called Blue Belle. The first time he entered his horse, he invited me to go with him. I met him at the track; he was giving it the "full treatment": checkered suit, the hat, the racing form.

He was dressed the part. His horse was entered in the fourth race — it was a six-horse race. As we were standing in line to place a small bet on Blue Belle (it was a token bet), his practice time assured us he couldn't win. A fellow in front of us was saying in a loud voice, "I'll bet $500 Blue Belle wins!" My friend and I were stunned, but didn't say anything because the fellow had been drinking quite heavily. As the horses went to post, this same fellow hurried to the betting window again. He was just able to walk; he was tight. At the top of his voice he said, "I want to bet $1000 on Blue Belle to win."

My friend went up to the drunken man and said, "Friend, I wish you wouldn't bet all that money on Blue Belle to win. You see, he can't win — I ought to know cause I own him." The drunk turned to my friend and said, "Well Buddy, this is going to be a slow damn race, because I own the other five."

Life is an individual proposition, and if you don't take advantage of the vital 5%, or if you're not prepared for the vital 5%, you blame yourself. How many times have you said, "Should I or shouldn't I?" Indecision is the graveyard for desires. It's the end of the line on your road to success and happiness.

You plan, you study, you're ready to take advantage of the vital 5%, then something happens. You become timid, backward, and you start thinking of all the reasons why you can't, when all you need is one reason why you can. The fault is within you, for you determine what you want and where you want to be. I have seen and I know you have seen countless people on the threshold of opportunity, but they procrastinated. They forget that they are part of the Creator, and that divine guidance is ever-present for the asking.

THE DAY THAT PASSED AWAY

Sometimes I get to thinking
Of the day that passed away,
I didn't accomplish anything.
T'was the day I didn't try.

I can't believe God put me here
To waste my time this way;
I'm sure He wanted an effort
In the game of life we play.

It's easy to promise ourselves
Tomorrow I'll start anew.
Tomorrow comes and, sure enough,
We forgot what we said we'd do.

But now I've found the answer:
I'm going to follow through.
Each morning I'll ask myself
What would God want me to do.

—Roy Pinyoun

THE BREAKFAST

Looking out for one's safety has been the watchword for centuries; but it has never been the watchword of the leaders. A leader must face danger. He must take a chance and face the consequences.

Our world has changed and will continue to change for the betterment of mankind. With these changes our reservoir of leaders will increase, which in turn will make America a richer place to live. Change is essential for a progressive atmosphere.

A small Negro boy stood watching the balloon-man at the State Fair. Suddenly a blue balloon broke loose and sailed overhead. So many people were alerted that the balloon salesman thought it would be a good idea to let another go. So he let a huge yellow balloon loose, and then a white one.

The little Negro boy, who had been watching these balloons fly out of sight, finally said to the man:

"Hey mister, if you sent a black one up, would it go as high as the others?"

The balloon-man, with an assuring smile said, "Young man, it's not the color that counts — it's the stuff inside that makes it rise."

It's the stuff inside — how true that is. Speaking of stuff inside which includes dedication, reminds me of the following story.

Harold Conway of Boston represented the United States in the hammer throw in the Olympic Games. His bicep muscle on his right arm measured eighteen inches. His left arm was crippled and four inches shorter than the other. This arm had been broken thirteen times and would not heal well, and so was half the size of his right arm.

In the finals of the hammer throw he faced two Russians.

As he took the hammer for his last throw he was far behind the Russians.

As he walked into the circle, 100,000 fans were screaming. Harold Conway bowed his head slightly and in a whisper said, "God, help me to do my best."

Would you expect Conway to win with the physical handicap he had? Would you expect him to compete against the two Russians who were perfect physical specimens in a contest that required strength and coordination?

Harold Conway set a new world's record! How did he do it? He had an insatiable desire that wouldn't let him quit. He had learned the secret — to battle on and not give up. This is one of life's greatest secrets in anything you do — battle on, don't give up!

How did he do it? Dedication — total dedication.

There was a church that wanted to raise some money, so they decided they would have a church breakfast. Heading up the committee was a chicken and a pig. The pig said, "I think it would be nice to have pancakes and eggs for the breakfast. I'm sure that as dedicated as the chicken is, she would be glad to donate some eggs." The chicken said, "I am dedicated to the church and I, like anyone else, would be more than glad to contribute to the cause. However, I think it would be more appropriate to have ham and eggs." The pig replied, "I appreciate your dedication by giving the church some eggs, but what you're asking from me is total dedication."

Well, the secret to all success is total dedication, but don't lose your head about it.

KEEPING ON

The mark of a man is what he'll do
When things aren't breaking his way.
It's easy to quit and forget the task
And wait for another day.

Success isn't easy, for everyone wants it
You must have courage and grit,
The one who succeeds is the one who says,
I'll keep going, I'll never quit.

When finally you arrive and success is yours,
Your battle has just begun.
For success is fickle, affections can change
It's courted by everyone.

So when you're on top, be proud of yourself,
But look for a goal beyond.
The secret of success in all that you do
Is simply, to keep keeping on.

—Roy Pinyoun

CARTER AIN'T COMIN'

Life is such that some of us tend to cringe or quit at the first sign of a crisis. We adopt the feeling of "what's the use" and turn our attention to something less trying. Perhaps it's human nature to take the path of least resistance, but that is not the path to success.

As Napoleon Hill has said, "every adversity has a seed of equivalent success." It doesn't assure us that success is going to be waiting for us — we must continue forward with a positive mental attitude, knowing that our efforts will be rewarded. This one fact answers the question why some men or women are successful. They kept on keeping on. I saw a badge the other day that had KOKO KLUB printed on it. I asked what it stood for. The man smiled and said, "Keep on keeping on."

Most of our failure today can be attributed to quitting, just plain giving up. It's the easiet thing to do, just quit.

I'm reminded of the story of a blind boy from Northwestern University. He would take notes in class in the Braille system shorthand. Then when he got back to his room he would type them and sell them to his classmates who could see. They had stronger eyes, but a weak ambition. This young blind man could have quit and perhaps no one would have blamed him. He didn't think of all the ways he couldn't attend college, he thought of the ways he could. It's simply whether you're going to think positively or negatively.

Regardless of who you are, whatever your ambition in life is, you must program your life. You must have direction and you must have a time table. When we put the men on the moon we had them programmed all the way up and all the way back. There was no guess work. We knew what would happen, because it was planned that way. Are you programmed? Do you have a destination? Do you know when you'll arrive? If you don't, now is the time!

It all starts with your thinking of what you are, what you can do and this, coupled with a positive approach, spells success.

The important thing is what you are within. Everything without is mirrored from within. All your desires, thoughts, and wishes make up your all-important world. Whether you color your world with ugliness or beauty, happiness or sorrow, it all has to come from within. By your own thinking you charter your life. Your reflection outside is a reflection of your world within. It is common knowledge whatever you think will, eventually, determine what you are, how you are, and what you do. You are the sum total of your thinking.

George Bernard Shaw says, "People blame circumstances, I like the person who looks for the circumstances he wants; if he can't find them, he makes his own."

A couple drove up to the Bonneventure Hotel in Montreal, Canada. The wife said she'd go and see if they had accommodations. She immediately came back and said, "They do not have any rooms." The husband said, "Come with me, they always have rooms; I'll get one." The husband walked up to the girl who was the room clerk and said, "We've come all the way from Raleigh, North Carolina; we're tired and need a room. The young clerk replied, "I'm sorry we have no rooms." The young fellow walked away and then turned around and said, "Young lady, if President Carter walked through that door and wanted to stay here tonight, would you find him a room?" The young girl smiled and said, "I guess if President Carter wanted to stay here tonight, we'd find him a room." The young man said "That's great, 'cause he ain't comin', give me his room." He was thinking.

LOVE

Babe Ruth, who many say was the greatest baseball player who ever lived; had an obsession for eating. The bat boy for the New York Yankees idolized Babe Ruth. Whatever Babe wanted the bat boy would get it for him. One day, Babe asked the bat boy to get him some hot dogs and coke. The bat boy ran to the concession stand and brought back ten hot dogs and seven cokes. Babe gulped them down and went for batting practice.

Later that day, Babe came down with a bellyache that was heard around the world. He was rushed to the hospital where he remained for a week. Babe's illness made the papers all over the world. Japan sent a reporter over to personally check on Babe's condition.

When the Yankees found out what happened, they fired the bat boy — the bat boy who had idolized Babe Ruth and who had dreams of becoming a baseball player. The bat boy never realized his dream of becoming a big league baseball player. However, he did reach the top in the movie industry. His name was William Bendix.

Willian Bendix loved Babe Ruth and because of this devotion he lost his job as mascot. William Bendix said, later in life, that he thought his world had ended when he could not be near the Babe.

Love is one of the strongest emotions. This story illustrates it.

There was a group of scientists in Chicago which was experimenting with moths. A female moth of rare species was placed in a room while four miles away a male moth of the same species was released. In a few hours the male moth was found beating its wings against the window of the room in which the female was confined. This experiment proved that there was some communication. Of course love might have been the motivating force that kept the male on her wave length.

I am reminded of a flight I had from Baltimore to Chicago.

We had leveled off at an altitude of twenty-five thousand feet, when I looked at the passengers I was sitting next to. I thought it was a mother and her little boy, but I wasn't sure. After another few moments, I turned to the mother and said, "What is that?" "What is that!" exclaimed the mother, "That's my son." She was rather upset that I should ask her. "Well, lady," I said, "I've seen ugly babies in my day, but you've got an award winner, a real blue ribbon winner." I thought the plane was going to explode when she started in on me. "Why, you low down specimen of a man! How dare you insult me! Oh, if I wasn't holding this baby I'd beat you to a pulp. You're not going to get away with this; I'm going to sue you and I'm going to sue this airline. I have never been so humiliated in my life." About this time, the stewardess, who had been up with the pilot, entered the cabin. She ran to the upset woman and said, "What on earth is the matter? Can I help you?" The lady yelled, "I'm going to sue this man; I'm going to sue the airline. I've never been so humiliated in my life." "Lady, lady, please calm down. Let me tell you what I'm going to do. I'm going to get a pillow for your head, a glass of iced tea for you and I'll see if I can find a banana for your monkey."

They say if you sit on the "lid of love, you'll be blown to pieces." Here's a story of a girl who was trying too hard to remove this lid.

This Catholic girl was going with a Protestant young man. This was a concern to the young lady's mother. The mother said to the daughter, "If he really loves you, he'll join the Catholic Church; but you must sell him on it." So the girl did do a good job and the young man said he'd join the Catholic Church. The mother was overjoyed and started to make preparations as mothers do. A few days later, the daughter came running into the house with tears streaming down her face, sobbing, "It's all over." The mother was shocked and reminded the girl that she said everything was wonderful and that he was going to join the Catholic Church. "Yes, Mother, everything was fine. I did sell him on becoming a Catholic, but I over-sold and he's going to become a Catholic priest!"

THE HELPER

Mrs. Bobbie Smith and her son, Jeff, were taking their English sheep-dog to the veterinarian for a minor operation. After the operation the "vet" suggested they hold the dog as he was still a little unsteady from the local anethesia. Mrs. Smith put the dog between her and Jeff, and proceeded to drive home. As they were driving down the highway, the dog began moving. Mrs. Smith momentarily took her eyes of the road to see if the dog was all right. As she did, the car swerved and careened off the highway, turning the car upside down. When the car came to a rest she immediately looked for Jeff. She found him pinned underneath the front end of the car. Jeff was screaming, "Mother, mother, I can't get my breath, please help me!" Mrs. Smith was five feet, two inches tall and weighed one hundred and five pounds. The thoughts that raced through her mind were frightening. She didn't have time to go for help. She couldn't possibly lift the front end of that car! Mrs. Smith said later, "I turned to God, and prayed as I went to the front of the car. I had heard of miracles, now I was asking for one. I put my hands under the front bumper and said, "Please Lord." The next thing I knew Jeff was putting his arms around me."

How did Mrs. Smith lift the front end of the car? This is another of the unanswered phenomena of the locked-up power we have at our disposal. Our bodies and minds are powerful things when guided by faith, prayer, and effort. Mrs. Smith had no other choice, but prayer, faith, and effort. God works in mysterious ways in the miracles He performs.

There was an elderly lady who lived at the foot of a mountain in Banning, California. She hated the mountain, so she decided she'd do something about it. When she went to bed that night she asked the Lord to remove the mountain. The next morning she was up at the crack of dawn to see if her prayers had been answered. Seeing the mountain still there, she remarked, "I knew it, I gave Him His chance, but I knew all the time there was nothing to this prayer business."

This is a pleading prayer, where she put on God's shoulders a responsibility she should assume. She should have faced this so-called problem with a prayer for tolerance.

We never know how we fit in and how much He is going to ask of us. We do know we will be called upon. So when a crisis faces you, remember God is testing you, as he tests others. He waits for a display of faith, courage and determination — for victory! This all is for naught without the toil and sweat that must encompass faith, courage and determination.

There is a story of some farm boys sliding down the roof of the barn onto a pile of hay. During the lunch break, one of the farm hands had moved the pile of hay, unbeknown to the boys. As the first boy went sliding down the roof, he noticed the hay had been removed. His only savior had to be the Lord, so he prayed. "Oh Lord, can you help me?" About that time his suspenders caught on a nail that was holding one of the gutters. The boy was left dangling off the edge of the barn roof. After regaining his senses, he said, "Oh Lord, I'm most grateful, but I didn't expect such sudden service." Once more, there is no difficulty that you cannot overcome. A wise old Negro once said, when asked how he overcame his difficulties, "How do I get through a trouble? First I try to go around it. If I can't, I try to go under it. If I can't, I try to go over it. If I can't go over it, then I gets my helper, the Lord, and we plow right through it."

THE SAW

There was a local science teacher who lived with an elderly bishop. Every night after they were through eating they would sit around and go over the happenings of the day. One night the young science teacher said to the bishop, "I believe that someday we will be traveling on a wagon that's propelled by fuel and will go much faster than the horse can go. I also believe that we will be talking to people by the means of wires, perhaps ten miles from here, maybe hundreds of miles." He stopped for a moment and then he said, "I also believe that someday man will be flying through the air." This was too much for the bishop who then said, "Young man, if you don't control your thinking and your tongue, you are going to have to move." Incidentally, that elderly bishop had two sons — Orville and Wilbur!

Today, as then, there are people who are not abreast of the times. They work for today, they live for today — never realizing that progress is essential for good growth, both individually and nationally. It's constantly being aware of the opportunities that we have to learn to improve our lust for life.

It's like the fellow who was cutting wood with a hand saw to make a living for his wife and family. One day a salesman asked him how much wood he cut a week, and the fellow replied, "About three truck loads, but that's if I work hard." The salesman said, "You come down to my store tonight and I'll let you use a saw for the next week; I promise you, you'll cut twice as much and you won't be half as tired." So the next week the fellow used the new saw, but he didn't cut any more wood and he was three times as tired as he'd ever been. After two weeks of using the new saw he was disgusted and took it back to the store. The salesman was astonished and said, "You mean you didn't cut any more wood?" "That's right,'' he replied. ''Besides, I'm so tired, I go to bed as soon as I get home at night.'' The salesman said, ''Bring the saw out to the back of the store and let's try it.'' The salesman pulled the cord on the saw and the saw went Buzzzzzzzzzzzzzzzzzzzz! The fellow looked at the saw and said, ''What's that noise?''

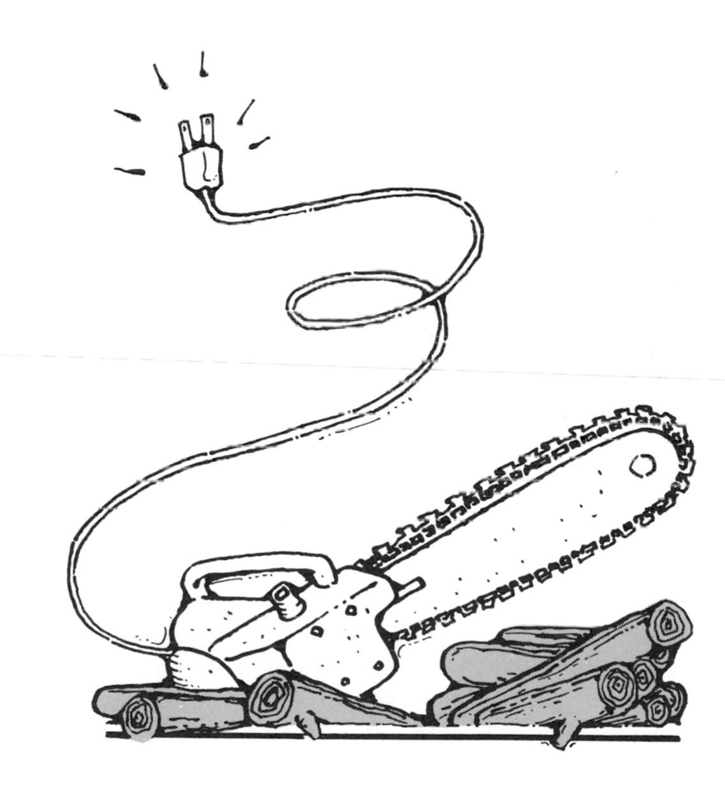

COUNTERFEIT

The authenticity of this can be found in the Congressional Record of 1875.

"A new source of power called gasoline had been produced by an engineer from Boston. This fuel is exploded in an engine, a so-called internal combustion engine. It is the belief of this committee that we are confronted with a problem that needs immediate attention. The potential danger could affect the entire world and most certainly the peace.

"Horseless carriages propelled by gasoline could possibly attain speeds of 15 to 20 miles per hour. The danger to our people of having these horseless carriages racing through our streets calls for immediate action."

The next time you think things are against you, remember Henry Ford — of the obstacles he had to overcome. He was experimenting in a virgin field, without money, and public opinion was against him.

Henry Ford was laughed at, ridiculed and despised for bringing forth his smelly, noisy, horseless carriage. At the height of all this animosity, he said, "I'll belt the world with an economical car." Henry Ford did just that. A poor, uneducated mechanic at forty, a billionaire at sixty, because he was thinking and he knew his thinking was right.

When you try something different, some people will laugh at you: expect it. A great man once said, "What the fool cannot understand he laughs at, thinking that by his laughter he shows superiority instead of being an idiot."

In the year of 1903 James Couzens told his sister about an automobile business organized by a mechanic named Henry Ford. He said he was going to be the office manager and urged her to invest $200. She didn't believe in the project, but did invest $100. Couzens, on the other hand, believed in Henry Ford. He borrowed $2,400 and with his sister's $100 they acquired 25 shares or 2½% of the company's first stock issue. Later Couzens was able to acquire 11½% of the total stock.

In the next sixteen years his sister's investment brought her $95,000 in dividends before she sold out to Henry Ford for $260,000. Couzens shares brought him $5,000,000 in dividends, and when he sold his stock to Henry Ford he received $30,000,000. The twelve original stock holders invested $28,000 and earned $250,000,000.

Bernard Baruch once said, "Don't sell the American dream short, there will always be opportunities for the thinking, well-disciplined man."

Today we are selling more automobiles than ever. Higher prices for them and the understanding that fuel prices will be $1.00 per gallon fail to dampen the American desire for comfort.

There is the story of a wealthy Englishman who wanted to purchase an American car. The salesman said, "My good man, we only have two American autos on the floor and we have a long waiting list." "That's dreadful," said the buyer. As the buyer left he tossed a large bundle of bills in the waste basket, to the amazement of the salesman. The next morning an automobile was delivered to him. However, later that day the salesman called and in a screaming tone said, "That money you threw in the waste basket was counterfeit." "Exactly," agreed the buyer, "that's why I threw it in the waste basket."

THANK YOU

I had to take the subway in from Forest Hills to Manhattan. It was early in the morning and as usual it was crowded. I was pushed, shoved, and finally ended up near the door. Without any place to sit I had to content myself with holding on to one of the straps suspended from the ceiling. As I did I was looking at a most beautiful woman, a person who had been beautiful in her early years and who as the years drifted by, had retained her beauty. I'm sure you've seen women like that, the type that has a glowing warmth and, as the time goes, reaches her peak in the early forties.

After I overcame the initial impact of her beauty, I stared as much as I dared. I stared unashamedly. I thought nothing wrong with a bit of innocent staring when it was motivated by admiration. There were no immoral thoughts. Perhaps this is the price a woman must pay for her beauty. For the next few minutes we swayed back and forth as the train headed for Manhattan. As we swayed our bodies almost touched. Above all I was a true gentleman, yet I wanted her to know I was enjoying her sheer beauty. As the train came to a stop, the doors rolled open. As they opened, getting on was one of the most beautiful young ladies I have ever seen. She was in her very early twenties. She was wearing a blue linen suit, that did absolutely nothing to hide her magnificent figure. She was in all probability a model. She had a shoulder bag draped across her shoulder. Her make-up was in the best taste, she was a picture of flawless beauty.

The only space available was next to the older beauty. This made a smashing picture! Here were the three of us, so close. Now, when someone that young and beautiful is so near, you look — and I looked. Believe me, I did notice all her charms. Suddenly the older woman seemed to tense a bit. Yet there was no show of emotion. I'm sure I knew what was going through her mind. I looked at the young girl and then my eyes flashed at a distance down the train. Then once more I turned back to the young girl, but just for a second. Then slowly all my attention was on the older lovely brunette. So as we headed for the city, my attention was solely on the older woman. As we were approaching Rockefeller Plaza, I knew I would never see the gorgeous brunette again. So I stared the longest and boldest stare. During the entire trip she had never looked at me in the eye, nor did she now. But now, as she brushed by me there was a slight smile on her face. I'm sure she felt she had been successful over the young beauty. For in those few minutes the three of us traveled together, my attention had been to the older brunette and now she was leaving. She was smiling as she passed by. Then in a very low voice she said, "Thank you." It was absolutely marvelous. Nothing more had to be said, it was there, all summed up in those two words. I'm sure it made the day for both of us.

Western Union says that people spend millions of dollars every year just to say thank you. Yet we can say it for nothing. Develop the habit of saying thank you to everyone. Thank you can't be said too much. People like to be thanked. They feel they're being appreciated and this makes them feel important and everyone wants to feel important. So, when a thank you is in order, say it. Who do you say it to? To everyone, from the boss to the garbage man. Nothing spreads happiness like a sincere thank you.

There is the story of the voluptuous blonde who was given a full-length mink coat by her elderly "Sugar Daddy." As she tried the coat, on, her admirer sat in anticipation of a token reward. She paraded back and forth caressing the expensive mink coat, when a sad look appeared on her face. "What's the matter, don't you like it?" inquired the "Sugar Daddy." "Yes," she replied, "but I was feeling sorry for the poor thing that was skinned." "Thank you," said the generous one.

When defining the qualities that a person should have for a

top job, the list is almost sure to include character, integrity, competitive spirit and leadership. Perhaps heading the list would be the ability to get along with people. To me, getting along with people is everything. To have their admiration, respect and loyality is the nucleus of a hard team to beat. How do you get along with people? By being appreciative, by listening to their plans, wishes and desires, and lastly and most important, saying "thank you."

Whatever you are, whatever you're doing, whoever you're with, people are primarily concerned with their own interests.

At sales meetings, in the classroom, or in a social gathering, people "light up" when you discuss something of importance to them. It is this "lighting up" or glowing enthusiasm that plays such an important part in our success structure.

The speaker, who is able to put the glow in a person's face and heart, has reached the ultimate. For what is more important than a happy glowing heart and face?

A psychiatrist was speaking to a group of Indians on the University of Iowa Campus. This speaker was enumerating the improvements the Indians were going to receive. The Indians, both young and old, educated and uneducated, were all impressed. When the speaker was finished, he slowly walked across the campus. A little, poorly clad Indian tugged on the speaker's coat sleeve and in broken English said, "I like best when I'm with you."

A teacher was asking her fourth-graders what they thought of their daddys. As you can imagine, the answers were quite plentiful. "I like my Dad because he takes me camping or he plays ball with me or he let's me go fishing with him." On this particular day, a boy, a bit small for his age, was frantically waving his hand for attention. The teacher finally said, "Yes, Billy." "I like my Daddy," he said, "because he plays with me; but most of all, when I help him work around the house, he says 'thank you, big guy.' I know then that I'm a big help and I'm a big guy."

Play like children everyday. Your neighbors may laugh at you, but your children will love you.

FEAR

Everytime you face a situation that seems impossible, you go through torture. Once you have faced it and gone through it, you are forever free of that fear.

Fear is one of the most powerful of all emotions and every fear is a fear of losing something.

If you dig deep enough you'll find the basis of every fear is the fear of loss. Loss of money — loss of health — loss of security — loss of job — loss of home — loss of so many things that in all probability, you'll never lose.

A great executive once said, "In business you must have courage; other business traits can be taught." "Courage," he went on, "is a matter of facing dangers and learning that when faced, they become less intimidating."

George Allen, the successful coach of the Washington Redskins, believes in giving his players a thorough understanding of the fundamentals, a thorough understanding of the plays and of the conditioning program he wants them to follow. He can give his players everything they need except the courage to do it. Knowing this, George Allen put a sign over the locker room door where everyone could see it. It read: "We give you everything but the guts to go out and do it!"

I was brought up on a farm on the outskirts of Cleveland, Ohio called South Euclid. I went to school at Charles F. Brush High School. I had to take the school bus in to school everyday. Before I got to the school bus I had to walk a mile up a dirt road to where the bus stopped. In the afternoon, I would take the school bus home and walk the mile down the road. When I started in Junior High, I began to notice the difference between boys and girls. Oh, I had noticed it before, but now I wanted to talk with them and walk them home from school. In fact, I would go into South Euclid which was close by and socialize with the girls there, too. This meant that I would miss the school bus home. Now, I had a transportation problem: how was I going to get home? Of course I could get a ride to the end of the road I lived on — and I always did. Then I had that mile walk down the dirt road to my house. In the daylight it was a pleasant walk, but at night, it was very dark; inky blackness all the way. It was not much of a road, just two ruts with the foliage high on each side. I would look down that road and I would be scared to death. I was a chicken. It wasn't that I was afraid of being alone, I was afraid that I wasn't. Then I would run all the way home as fast as my feet would carry me. When I reached home, I'd sit on the front porch, beads of perspiration running down my face, and I'd say, "I made it again."

When I became a junior in High School, they elected me Captain of the basketball team. I knew if the fellows thought I was afraid to walk down that road they would lose respect for me. So I promised myself the next time I was confronted with that problem I would *walk* down that road. Sure enough, a few nights later, I was looking down that long, dark road. I was still a "chicken" but I was determined to walk. So I decided, that inasmuch as I was going to walk, I'd walk on my tip toes and I did. I walked down this road, and as I took two steps on the bridge that was half-way between the main road and my house, someone said, "Who's there?" By that time, there wasn't anyone. I ran home, sat on the front porch and I was petrified. After I calmed down and my senses returned, I realized that that was my drinking cousin. He had been to South Euclid and had too many beers. As he walked or swayed down the dirt road and came to the bridge, he had seen two bridges and he had walked between them.

To me, this was one of the greatest revelations of my life. It was a lesson that has stayed with me all these years: that if you face up to fear and conquer it, it will never come back to haunt you. After this episode, I could walk down that road and nothing seemed to bother me. I had become the master of fear.

The late Mr. Barnum had the solution to whip fear. He'd be confronted by a fear and he'd say, "I'm going to sleep; I can't do anything about it." He'd wake up refreshed, ready to tackle any problem.

We are always going to have some problems and troubles; it's necessary for a good tough growth. It's like the young man to whom, after his wedding, the minister said, "Son, you are at the end of your troubles." A few years later, he threatened to beat up the preacher. "Why?" asked the preacher. "You said I was at the end of my troubles," replied the young man. "Well, you were," replied the preacher, "but I didn't say which end."

WISH

When I was growing up, I spent a great deal of time fishing. Many times airplanes would fly over and I would wish I could someday fly in one of those airplanes. At last my dream has been fulfilled, for I fly a great deal. Now as I'm flying and I look down, I wish I were fishing.

I think we all wish we could slide the years back and do things we did as a child, for a little while anyway. There is nothing wrong with wishing as long as it doesn't distort our outlook on life. The evil of wishing is wishing for what someone else has and not being willing to work for it.

A philosopher once wrote "There is not much to do, but bury a man when the last of his dreams are dead." This is the answer to staying young; some people are old at forty, others are young at ninety.

There is an old cliché that says, "Shoot for the moon; you might hit a star." It's this pursuing of something just beyond our reach that makes life worth while, and although we never reach it, we'll be a better person because we tried.

A person is as young as his dreams and as old as his doubts, for age is a figment of the mind.

Speaking of age: A sales manager was urging his men to try increasing the volume of their accounts.

"Once upon a time," he said, "a sultan had twenty beautiful wives. He would sit on his throne and when he had selected the wife he wanted, he'd send a ten year-old boy, called a "runner," after her. Time went on, and the sultan lived to be one hundred-twenty-one years old, while the runner died at forty. Gentlemen, business never hurt anyone — it's the running after it that wears men out."

It has been said that there are two things to aim at in life: first, to get what you want, and after that, to enjoy it. Only the wisest achieve the second.

We are brought into this world and our parents "do" for us. Everything we need, they do for us. When we go to school, the teachers do the teaching and our family does the training at home. It is always someone else "doing." After we leave school we have the task of finding our life's work. For the first time we realize that we must "paddle the boat." We now must start "doing" and for this "doing" we will be compensated.

A salesman noticed an ad in a magazine that read "How To Get Rich." All he had to do was send two dollars and they would send him the secret. The salesman immediately sent the two dollars and anxiously waited to get the secret of how to get rich. A week later, his letter arrived and he ripped the envelope open and there was a card with one word on it — WORK!

The salesman was disappointed, but he still looked through the various magazines hoping to find another solution on how to get rich. Finally, in big print, "How To Get Rich Without Working." The salesman was over-joyed. [This had to be his answer.] He sent the two dollars they asked, then waited patiently. A few days later, his letter came. He ripped it open, and the answer was "Do what we're doing!"

Unfortunately, too many people today are still waiting for people to do things for them.

It's like our friend Bill who met his good friend Jim at a midget league baseball game. He said, "Jim, I'm glad to see you. I need $500.00." Jim said, "I don't know, Bill; that's a lot of money." Bill said, "But Jim, do you remember when your daughter was very sick, and I gave her a quart of blood? Do you remember when we were in the Viet Nam war and you were wounded and I faced enemy bullets to drag you back to safety? Then there was the time you and your wife had an argument and you had a knife at your wife's throat and I took it away from you? Listen to me, Jim, I saved your life, your daughter's life, and your wife's life."

"That's true, Bill; but what have you done for me lately?"

THE BUSY MAN

I knew a man who was wealthy;
Who went to his office each day;
Folks thought he was eccentric,
Because he took no time to play.

He'd be meditating and thinking,
As he'd hustle down the street.
T'was a wave, or a quick "hello"
For the people he'd chance to meet.

He was busy every hour of the day.
His business, few people knew;
But he was judged by other people's thoughts,
None of which were true.

Yet the man they labeled eccentric,
Was helping others — they didn't know
Of his love for his fellow man.
He was too busy to tell them so.

—Roy Pinyoun

It has always perplexed me how people can make a hasty judgment on what they imagine, when all it would take is a little time and effort to see what really is.

Woodrow Wilson summed it up when he said, "One cool judgment is worth a thousand hasty councils. The thing to do is supply the light and not the heat."

In the war of succession between France and England in the year 1756, a vessel was found ship-wrecked one morning. There was only one survivor. The English people did not recognize the survivor, but in fear of who he might be they had a trial and convicted the defendant of being a spy. His sentence, that he be hanged, was carried out. The spy later was found to be a gorilla.

It seems that Maw and Paw came into town once a month to get their staples. It was a long ride over the mountain which separated their valley cabin from the town. This particular day there was a train in town and it created quite an interest, as Maw and Paw had never seen one. Paw went up and touched it, surveyed the length of it and shook his head. "'Twill never move, never move," he said. About that time the conductor yelled, "All aboard!" the train got up a head of steam and gradually moved down the tracks. Maw turned to Paw and said, "Well, what do you think now?" Paw shook his head, looked at Maw and said, "It'll never stop; it'll never stop."

THE NEIGHBORHOOD

Christopher Columbus, who is given credit for discovering America, was courageous, for he never quit. To finance his voyage he appealed to his home state of Genoa. He also contacted Henry II of England. He was rebuked at every turn.

During one of the committee meetings, where a discussion was being held as to the plausibility of his trip, an interesting new member appeared. The new member was outspoken and suggested they immediately make arrangements to initiate a trip to the New World. This rashness angered the other committee members. After all, the other committee members were the finest minds that could be assembled with experience in varied fields all pertaining to the voyage.

The new member was dismissed and the explanation was as follows. "Inasmuch as you were a replacement for one of the original committee members, we feel that in the short time you have been here your thinking is of an immature nature. The fact that you were in favor of the voyage immediately shows lack of stability. Some of the members feel you are eccentric with delusions and fantasies. It has been found you imagine yourself to be an artist. The idea of "flying machines," which you talk about, definitely proves your thinking is of a dangerous nature."

This new member was an illegitimate son of a Florentine official. He took his name from his birthplace, Vinci; Leonardo was his first name. Leonardo da Vinci and Columbus had every reason to forsake their dreams. Both have filled pages in our history books on shear courage alone. da Vinci, as a child, was chided by his friends, because of his birth. At an early age da Vinci vowed that he would be recognized. He was that; he is thought of as the finest painter Italy ever had — many maintaining the greatest in the world.

Later in life, the nobility, even Kings and Queens requested his presence at social functions. da Vinci once said, "Oh God what you give for the price of an effort." We are all blessed with an unlimited supply of effort, an infinite supply is always available — it is at our command.

In Johnstown, Pennsylvania, during one of the floods, effort prevailed to save a precious piano. Two men carried the heavy instrument up a narrow stairway in the face of a swift-rising flood. When the water subsided, it took six men to take the piano down.

It's heart-warming to read about people who have overcome seemingly unsurmountable obstacles. There's the story of the boy who was born of poverty-stricken parents in the city slums. He married a neighborhood girl and they had several children. He was a hard worker and finally became wealthy. He acquired factories, rental property, and oil wells. He had a home in Palm Springs and a mountain retreat. It is reported that his yacht cost one half million dollars. But he never forgot the crummy neighborhood where he was brought up. Once a year he goes back and visits his wife and children.

IT'S THE DECISIONS!

Abraham Lincoln's mother was dying. Abe was kneeling by the bed holding her hand, and as he looked at his mother he realized that here was a true pioneer — she had plowed the fields, split rails, built fences, helped build their cabin and did all the chores in the house. What Abe remembers most was her teaching him all she knew. Just before his mother died she looked up and said to Abe, "Be somebody, be somebody!" Abe said he never forgot his mother's last words. Abraham Lincoln had to have a motivating force, for problems, defeats and frustrations stayed with this man throughout his life. Seven times he was defeated while running for office. He fell in love with a young lady, only to watch her die from typhoid fever. He tried to get a position with the United States land office, this too failed. He went in business but went bankrupt, taking him seventeen years to pay off his debts. "Be somebody" made a believer of Abe, for he knew if he kept trying long enough, the pendulum of success had to swing his way.

Abe enjoyed playing baseball. He was playing one day when a group of politicians ran excitedly up to him and said, "Abe you've been nominated for the Presidency of the United States." Abe said, "Gentlemen, gentlemen, step back a bit until I get my licks at bat."

Abe's love of children, his courageous attitude and his dedication to the ideals and principles he believed, were finally rewarded by his being president of the United States.

We all should take heed to "be somebody"; of course we can't all become presidents, but we can all "be somebody" to the best of our abilities. The trouble is too many people wait; they wait for the Spring, they wait for the Summer, then the Fall and Winter. They keep waiting and wishing, wanting and wondering, plotting and planning, dreaming and hoping and praying for something to happen. What they don't realize is — you have to make it happen! Abe Lincoln made it happen — he kept trying, he was determined to "Be somebody!" Each of us have that decision to make: are we willing to pay the price?

It's like the tramp who asked the farmer for work. The farmer said, "My wife's flowers need weeding; you can start doing that if you really want to work." The tramp was finished in a short time. The farmer was pleasantly surprised and said, "My wife could use a few quarts of blackberries for tonight." The tramp finished the job and reported back to the farmer. The farmer then showed the tramp some potatoes he had in the basement and told him he wanted them graded into three piles, small ones, medium ones, and large. The farmer left, and finally after four hours went into the basement to see what was keeping the tramp so long. The farmer said to the tramp, "I'm surprised you're not finished. What's keeping you so long?" "Oh," said the tramp, "it's hard for me to make these decisions."

YOU

Some Russians are born, reared, and die and have never gone more than ten miles from their birthplace. The average salary in Russia is $134 per month. The Russian rulers print what they want them to read, tell them where they will work, tell them where they will live and tell them what to worship.

In America we are blessed with all the freedoms; freedom of religion, press, speech, and the freedom of the pursuit of happiness — our happiness.

An appropriate story is told about the Russian commissar who was traveling around to the various villages holding meetings, telling how good things were: "Why, the Russians are eating better, they are wearing better clothing, and everyone is happy," he said. Before closing his address he asked, "Is there anyone here who wants something?" A fellow in the back raised his hand. The commissar said, "Stand up, state your name, and what it is you want."

"My name is Shapiro, Shapiro is my name, and I want a TV," he said.

The commissar said, "Ah ha, you want a TV — you'll get it."

One year goes by, the same commissar comes back, has the meeting, and tells the people how fortunate they are. Before closing he says, "Is there anything you want?"

A fellow in the back raises his hand.

Commissar says, "Stand up, state your name, and what it is you want."

"My name is Katz," he said, "Katz is my name. Whatever happened to Shapiro?"

The most precious thing any one can have is freedom. It is as fragile as a tulip and as beautiful. It is the essence of what our forefathers fought for, a heritage we should be proud of and protect at any cost. So fragile, so beautiful, and so precious that we should devote our lives appreciating and protecting what our forefathers gave us. For America is one of the few countries which is free in the true sense of the word.

We live in the richest country in the world. We live in a country where our dogs eat better than 90% of the people overseas. Sixty-two percent of the families overseas never sit down to a family meal and 72% of the people overseas have never gone to a dentist.

General Motors' gross output is more than all of Mexico's; and if New York and California could become countries, they would be the sixth and seventh largest producing countries in the world. The state of Illinois out-produces all of Africa, and our seven seaboard states out-produce all of Russia and Asia combined.

The brain, if it were duplicated, would take a building the size of the Empire State Building; the electrical system to function this brain would be equivalent to New York City's electrical supply; the air-conditioning system would be enormous and the Hudson river would have to be rechanneled to furnish the cooling. This wonderful brain of ours that can function for four hours on the energy from one peanut is remarkable. This brain of ours, with all its possibilities, baffles all attempts to evaluate it.

We are truly in the land of opportunity; and yet 50% of the people are so shackled with worries and troubles that they're bored with life.

Why do people remain bored with life? It's in their thinking.

Roman emperor, Marcus Aurelius, said 1800 years ago, "Our life is what our thoughts make it."

The average person contains: water — 10 gallons, fat — enough to make 7 bars of soap, carbon — enough to make 9,000 lead pencils, phosphorous — enough to make 2,200 match heads, magnesium — enough to make one dose of salts, lime — enough to whitewash one chicken coop, sulphur — enough to rid one dog of fleas; and all this can be reduced to ashes, that are worthless. They say we are worth 78¢ from the neck down. What we're worth from the neck up is how we think.

Whatever condition you are facing now is the result of your thinking, good or bad. If you want to change your conditions, first change your thinking.

You are the architect; you build your future. Things must first be fashioned in your mind. In short, the future success that you have is in your hands — *you* decide.

Sir Isaac Newton was asked how he discovered the law of gravitation. He replied, "By thinking about it all the time."

There is the secret! Think about it all the time.

In St. Louis, Missouri, I was presiding over a seminar. During one of the lectures I had said, "Your body's growth and development may come from what you eat, but your success or failure comes from within, by what you think. You literally become what you think about."

After the meeting a young fellow said to me, "All that nonsense about you becoming what you think about is not true. If that was true I'd have been a girl before I was twenty years of age."

Everyone has the right to all the knowledge he wants. If one pursues it long enough he'll realize that it is power when put to use. The more one searches for this knowledge, the more his thinking is stimulated; and if he puts action to this, his horizons are manyfold.

It is thinking of a positive nature that determines our world, our conditions and our surroundings.

At Kent State University, where I went to college, I had a professor write this on the blackboard. "Look for the best, believe the best and expect the best. This is how the door of miracles can be opened — they can be opened to you."

All our knowlege, our thinking, our actions go for naught if we don't have faith, if we don't believe.

First we must have knowledge, knowledge of the product, knowledge of the customer. At this point, it's imperative to mention that many buyers buy from the salesman rather than the company. Because the buyer knows the salesman and the salesman knows all about the buyer.

Once a man had ordered some merchandise but failed to pay for it. The merchant, who had sent the merchandise, wrote to the station agent, inquiring if the merchandise had been delivered. He also inquired from the local bank if the purchaser's credit was good. Being a thorough merchant, he wrote to the mayor of this small town for the name of a reliable lawyer.

Sometime later he received this letter:

Dear Sir: As station agent, I am glad to report that the so mentioned goods were delivered. As president of the local bank, I should like to inform you that my credit is good. As mayor of our town I can only recommend one lawyer because we only have one and that is me.

Furthermore, if I were not the pastor of our only church I would tell you to go to hell!"

There is not and never will be a substitute for knowledge. However, all the knowledge in the world isn't worth a hill of beans if we don't use it.

Sometime ago I went into a hardware store to buy a hammer. The young clerk thrust one in my hand and said, "That will be $2.75."

I said, "Do you have anything else?"

The clerk said, "Yes, we have one for $1.75."

"What is the difference?" I asked.

He said, "$1.00."

I was annoyed, so I went to another hardware store. I said, "I'd like to buy a hammer."

The salesman handed me a hammer and said, "Isn't that a good grip, can't you get a good hold on it?"

I said, "Yes."

"That handle is hickory, it will always be smooth. The hammer is stronger than any other hammer; it won't break. Also, the claws are reinforced and can pull out any nail without breaking. That's not all, this hammer will never lose its polish, and it's rust proof. The cost is only $2.75."

"Do you have any others?"

"Yes, this one is $1.75, but it could break if you drop it; it's cast iron. It's a very inferior hammer and so sells for less."

The difference is quite obvious; one clerk has the right attitude. He is using all his knowledge and giving 100%. This young man has a future, not because he works in a hardware store, but because he is utilizing all his talents for the benefit of the company. The other salesman, with his don't-care attitude, is doomed for a job of mediocrity. His future, as well as his sales pitch, is limited.

I'm not criticizing the first salesman, however. Too many people are looking for the cheap way out, and some people would immediately take the cheapest hammer.

I have a friend who wants everything wholesale. It's not that he doesn't have the money; he's retired and he's wealthy. He wouldn't buy the cheapest hammer; he'd shop around until he could get the best one wholesale.

There was an only child in a family and he was spoiled. He would disobey, he would break things and he would not mind his parents. One day he walked into the living room with a hammer and some nails. There were friends visiting this particular night. The little boy, who was six, walked over to the coffee table, took a nail out of his pocket, and proceeded to pound it into the coffee table. After he drove six nails in the coffee table, he climbed on the dining room table and continued to pound nails. The guests were surprised that the parents hadn't reprimanded the boy. Finally, one of the friends said, "Your son likes to pound nails in the furniture, doesn't he?"

"Yes," replied the father, "He does it all the time."

"Doesn't it get expensive?" the guest asked.

"Oh no," replied the father, "we get the nails wholesale!"

Yes, America symbolizes freedom — speech, religion, press, assembly — elections, travel, to publish this book — even to pound nails!

DEDICATION

Charles Atlas was a weakling. Then he became dedicated to building his body, and it became one of the most perfect bodies in the world. He has won almost every award and is recognized today as the foremost authority on body building — dedication!

Walter Chrysler is well known today because he dedicated his life to building a better automobile. When Walter Chrysler was a young man he was interested in engines. He saved his money and when he had $4,000 he bought the best automobile on the market at that time. He drove the automobile home and immediately started taking it apart. The neighbors thought he was crazy; they laughed at him, they ridiculed him, but Chrysler was dedicated. He had a goal and nothing could discourage him.

Chrysler's plan was constructive. If this was the best car on the market, he wanted to see why and how it was made. Then he would improve on it. This he did and brought forth the Chrysler automobile. All this happened because he was dedicated.

What does it take to become dedicated? It takes a goal. So let's all set a goal! Just a short term goal, so we can become goal conscious; then let's put an effort behind it. Too many people set goals and that's all they do. You must put action behind your goals.

There was an elderly gentleman watching a tennis match for the first time. He was amazed at the number of times the tennis ball hit the net. He said, "They should take the net down — then they wouldn't have to worry about the ball hitting the net!" Tennis is a game of skill, timing, and stamina. Part of the game is getting the ball over the net.

I was playing golf at the number two course in Pinehurst. It is a difficult course with trees lining the fairways and streams that ran across the course, and deep sand traps. I was playing in a foursome. My partner said, "I wish they would make this course easier." Take the net down; make the course easier! Competition and opportunity make a person grow.

Our great country developed because we had pioneers with a competitive spirit who relished the opportunity to push "westward." A good athlete, like our early frontiersmen, thrives on competition — the desire to accomplish, to succeed, to win. Of course you can't win all the time.

As Clemenceau said, "Life is interesting when you have failed, for it proves you have reached for something greater."

Disraeli said, "All my successes are the results of my failures." But try and try again, always with a positive mental attitude. These are the ingredients necessary for success.

I've always enjoyed going to Chicago, perhaps because it's a big city. I am from Raleigh, North Carolina, where we lack the entertainment that Chicago has. My opportunity always came when I went to the Restaurant Show, held annually on the Navy Pier. I would allot one night to go to the Palmer House to see their outstanding floor show. One particular night I hurried back to my room and dressed, hurrying to make the first show. I hurried up the stairs and waited for the maitre d' to seat me. When he finally turned around I said, "You've got a crowd tonight." "Yes," he said, "We're completely sold out." I walked away dejectedly, heading for my room. As I was about to get on the elevator, I saw my friend Earl Davis. Earl is one of the best salesmen I have ever known. He works for Hydeco, which sells pumps and accessories. He has been one of the leading salesmen for years. Other salesmen dislike him because he has that knack of selling and getting the things out of life that he wants. I hollered, "Earl! Earl Davis!" "Roy," he said, "What are you doing in Chicago?" After the formalities were over (I hadn't seen him in nine years) he said, "Let's go up and see the floor show!" My first reaction was to tell Earl that I had been up there and they were sold out. Then I decided for once I'll see Earl not get what he wanted. I said, "Good idea, Earl; lead the way." Up the same stairs we ran; I was anxious to see how Earl would handle the maitre d'. When we got to the door, Earl did not wait, he walked into the dining area as if he were looking for his table. I knew there wasn't any table — I had been told they were sold out. About this time the maitre d' sees Earl. Earl immediately holds up two fingers, meaning table for two. I am, at this point, embarrassed. To my surprise the maitre d' turns to a young fellow cleaning off the tables and holds up two fingers. This is telling the young fellow to find a table for two. To my utter amazement I saw this young fellow bring in a small table and place it right up front. He then hurried back and brought two chairs, and we sat down. I didn't say a word, I was completely in a state of bewilderment. I thought — I had just been up there — they were sold out — I only wanted one chair! Earl had once again taught me a lesson. When I originally approached the maitre d' I had inquired about business — I said "You've got a crowd tonight!" I didn't use a positive approach. On the other hand, Earl said, "Roy, let's go to the floor show." His attitude was positive and when he reached the dining area he acted positively. In retrospect, I was inquiring about business; Earl wanted to see the floor show. He was dedicated to what he wanted.

IT'S YOUR TIME

Orville and Wilbur Wright, two bicycle makers, made more than a thousand glider flights. On December 17, 1903, they made history when their first plane flew 120 feet. Their first flight was about the wingspan of a modern jet. Only a handful of people saw this first flight that ushered in an era, that skyrocketed beyond the imagination. In fifty years we have gone from Kitty Hawk to the jet.

Another man, whose name has long been forgotten, had developed and constructed an airplane and had it in his garage. History tells us that he flew it the day following the Wright Brothers eventful day at Kitty Hawk.

Why didn't he fly it before? Because he didn't believe. The principle of believing is like dialing a telephone. You get exactly what you dial. If you dial the wrong number, failure; failure is what you'll get. Without belief, there can be no successful outcome.

Dr. Norman Vincent Peale says, "You are or you become what you deeply believe. You never can be better, more successful or bigger than you believe you can be."

Millions of farmers every year scatter their grain with the belief that each grain will grow many more grains. If he plants wheat, he will harvest wheat; if he plants barley, he'll harvest barley. This is nature's law of productivity; you reap what you sow.

You have seen projectors which hold slides and the picture on the slide is reflected on a screen. If you put in a pretty picture of the ocean at sundown, it will be reflected on the screen. On the other hand, if you put in a picture of a family whose house has been burned to the ground, there wouldn't be a pretty picture on the screen.

You have two boxes of slides at your command. One box contains slides of faith, desire, determination, ambition, hope, love, and many other worthwhile slides. In the other box you have slides of defeat, cowardice, hate, fear, jealousy, and many other worthless slides. Which box of slides are you going to use to reflect on your screen of life?

The Wright Brothers made a wise selection — will you?

Whenever I talk about airplanes, I'm reminded of the story of our State Fair in Raleigh. There was a helicopter taking people up for rides. It was a pleasant ride where you could get a panoramic overview of this mammoth Fair. A farmer who was examining the helicopter was asked, "Would you like to take a ride?" "Nope," replied the farmer, "If the Lord meant for us to fly He would have given us wings." The pilot replied, "I can tell you're a religious man, so you must know that when your time comes you're going to die." The farmer took off his hat, scratched his head and said, "Reckon so, but what if we's flying up there and the Lord decides it's *your* time to go?"

I'D BEEN A JANITOR

There was a farm boy who decided he would rather stand behind a counter than a plow. He was not a salesman, in fact, no one would hire him. He began to think he was a misfit — but, he tried. Out of his first five stores, three failed — but he kept trying. This boy who kept trying was Frank W. Woolworth, who was destined to become one of the largest retail merchants in the world with a store in every city of 8,000 or more population.

I am telling you this story because I hear of people thinking of quitting simply because they have a few setbacks.

When you feel this way, stand in front of a mirror and have a serious talk with that person who looks back at you. All you have to do is change your attitude. Your attitude is made up of your wishes, hopes, and desires — and you certainly don't want negative wishes, hopes, and desires, do you? So change to positive wishes, hopes, and desires.

If you had a light bulb that burned out, you wouldn't sit around and weep about the fact that there is no light — instead, you would remedy the situation simply by installing a new bulb. This holds true with every negative thought you have. Don't dwell on the negative bulb. PS — You've got an unlimited supply always within you, so don't let your light go out.

We have seen opportunities come and go because the person was powerless in his ability to act. The indecision, the hesitancy, is one of the saddest things to come from the human heart — it sounds the death toll on all hope, ambition, self-confidence, initiative, and accomplishment.

Conrad Hilton, of the famous Hilton Hotels, says, "I encourage boldness because of the dangers of pension plans and security plans that tend to settle persons in ruts of complacency instead of trying to find their rainbow."

A group of businessmen had a survey taken in some of the leading colleges. One question was asked of the seniors: What do you want most out of graduation? Ninety-two percent said they wanted security most. They all said they were willing to start at the bottom of the ladder and work their way up. What the businessmen wanted were more young men who were willing to *hold the ladder.*

Conrad Hilton says he believes in dreaming big dreams. After all, in the beginning everything had to originate in the mind, in the form of a dream. From the dream comes your imagination, and from your imagination come the children, called ideas.

Adolph Zukor of Hollywood was asked what he attributed his amazing success to. He said he was fortunate to get in a growing business and to go along with the tide. As for the lesson he learned, he said, "Be grateful for your disappointments — without them you could not recognize accomplishments."

Have you noticed how many foreign people come to America and succeed? Do you know why they succeed? Because they have to. They don't have anyone to go to for help. They *have* to be successful.

There is the story of a young man in Athens who applied for a job in the school system as a janitor. Because he could not read or write, he didn't get the job. Some years later he came to America and worked as a laborer, saved his money and went to night school. The years rolled by and this Greek immigrant continued to work, save and study. His desire to find his place in America paid dividends, for he became a wealthy, respected man in his community. With his enthusiasm still glowing, he continued his pursuit of more and greater goals. Later in life this Greek immigrant was being honored at a banquet. He spoke in a very articulate and well poised manner — a far cry from his early days in New York City. In his speech he told of his early boyhood in Greece and how he lost his first job because he couldn't read or write. After his speech was over, a reporter came to him and said, "If you had been able to get an early education in Greece, there is no telling what you could have done." The honored man smiled and said, "If I had had an early education in Greece, I'd have been a janitor."

THE CHANDELIER

There is a saying, "Give a man a fish and he can eat for a day; show him how to fish and he can eat for a lifetime."

Knowledge is knowing about something; know-how is knowing how to do something. Knowledge is information; know-how is technique. You need both to succeed in life.

Knowledge can be obtained anywhere — from people, books, or by observing. It is necessary that you know *what* you want to know.

Perhaps one of the greatest assets to knowledge is to ask someone who can help you. The Bible says, "Ask and you shall receive" — you are promised that all you have to do is ask.

Psychologists tell us the reason people do things is to feel important. Everyone wants to feel important. When you ask someone something you are making them feel that you need them. This in turn makes them feel important. When they tell you what you wanted to know they are demonstrating their importance.

Marcus Aurelius, supposedly the Roman Empire's wisest ruler, once said, "I am going to meet people today who talk too much, people who are selfish, egotistical, and ungrateful. I shall not be surprised, however, for I could not imagine a world without such people." You will meet people like that, you will meet people who will not co-operate with you when you ask.

I'm reminded of the church committee that met and agreed unanimously to buy a new chandelier. The preacher thought it would be a nice gesture to tell the congregation about the committee's decision. One Sunday, after his sermon, he explained about the committee's decision to buy a new chandelier. To eliminate any misunderstanding, he said, "Would anyone like to comment on the board's decision?"

A little old lady stood up and said, "I question the decision of the committee. First, I don't think we can afford this new-fangled chandelier. Secondly, I don't think anyone knows how to play it. Thirdly, and most important, I question their decision — if we have any money at all why don't we get more light in the church by buying a new light fixture?"

THEY LAUGHED

Four thousand years ago someone invented the wheel; it was round and funny looking. Nobody had seen a wheel before, so they laughed.

In 1803 the first steamboat left from Albany, New York. A boy raced and beat it, and the people laughed.

In 1865 the first telephone was invented — but who wanted to talk to a bunch of wires. So they laughed.

In 1867 the first automobile went chugging down the street. The horse and buggy passed it as if it were standing still — and it usually was. And the people laughed.

In 1869 there was the first incandescent light — but the light was so dim they had to use a gas light to see. And the people laughed.

A new plan, scheme, idea or solution, many times will be greeted with laughter. A fool laughs at what he can't conceive. And I remember: "Someone said it couldn't be done; but he, with a chuckle, replied, 'maybe it couldn't, but he'd be one that didn't give in 'til he tried'." That is the spirit of a dynamic, positive person. The spirit of accomplishment, the spirit of setting a goal and working until it is reached.

Millet, the French painter, paid 50¢ for paint and brushes and 50¢ for a piece of canvas. On this piece of canvas he portrayed the greatness of his soul and gave the world a painting called "The Angelus," and it sold for $105,000.

We will always have the 'doers,' the 'doubters,' the 'I cants,' and the 'I wills.' It's the 'doer' who creates the circumstance. You either become the creator or the creature of. Be the cause, not the effect.

People can be divided into three groups. First, those people who make things happen. Then there are those who watch things happen. Then we have those who laugh at others and have no idea what has been happening.

There are many people who have no idea what's happening. I'm sure you'll agree this story sums it up.

Two of my business associates and I were just about to walk into the Hyatt House in Atlanta, Georgia. As we started up the steps, a gorgeous young lady who was too drunk to drive started to get into her new car. I said to Ronnie, "That young lady is going to kill herself or someone else. She is in no condition to drive." Then I said, "Ronnie, why don't you offer to drive her home?" Ronnie liked the idea, so he went over to the girl and suggested that he drive her home and then bring the car back to the Hyatt House. She could pick it up the following day. This she agreed upon. After helping her in the car (and she needed help), I got in the back seat and Ronnie sat beside our drinking lady friend. As we drove along, she looked up at Ronnie and smiled. A few minutes later she smiled and looked at Ronnie and said, "You're passionate." Ronnie winked at us and said, "Did you hear that? She said I'm passionate." A few minutes later she put her hand on Ronnie's leg and said, "Hey, you're passionate." Ronnie could hardly contain himself — the thought of having this gorgeous creature tell him he's passionate. We drove for another ten minutes and as we stopped at an intersection Ronnie said, "Where do you live?" She smiled and said to Ronnie, "I kept telling you, you were pashin' it." (passing it.)

ENTHUSIASM

Enthusiasm comes from the Greek word "entheos," which means *full of God.*

It's the tempo of all progress. It's the rhythm of all success. As Emerson said many years ago, "Nothing great today, tomorrow or of yesteryears was ever accomplished without enthusiasm."

It's the sparkle in your eyes; it's the grip of your hand; it's the way you walk and the way you talk — all of this makes up your degree of enthusiasm. This enthusiasm that you have is going to be reflected in the people that you come in contact with and in those who work for you.

You don't have to have enthusiasm, just like you don't have to have gasoline for an automobile. Now if you don't have gasoline, your car will have to be pushed. If you don't have enthusiasm, you'll have to be pushed and so will your people.

Ramsey McDonald, who was prime minister of England, was with his wife during her last few minutes as she was dying. Just before she died, she said, "Ramsey, try to fill the lives of our children with love and enthusiasm and you'll never have anything to worry about."

Joe Leonard of an eastern pharmaceutical company would hold a sales meeting every Saturday morning at the Statler Hotel. Everytime he had a new group of salesmen, he would walk amongst them and ask them, "What is salesmanship?" As they gave their answers, he would say, "That's good, that's all right, very good, that's good thinking. I like that." After this, he would say, "Let me tell you what I think salesmanship is. Salesmanship is the transfer of enthusiasm." From that day on, whenever the company had a sales meeting, he would stand in front of the salesmen and ask them what salesmanship was. Everyone together would yell, "it's the transfer of enthusiasm."

While I was reading in bed a few nights ago I said to my wife, Connie, "They're making the print in these books smaller." She said, "Roy, you need glasses."

The next morning I went to the optometrist. He gave me a thorough examination, charged me $35.00 and said, "You need glasses." My wife told me the same thing and she hadn't charged me $35.00. I thought *what a rip-off.* I finally turned to the doctor and asked, "Do I need them now?" "No," he replied, "You could get a seeing-eye dog." I hated him. I almost walked out. He couldn't be a good optometrist.

He put some drops in my eyes and I waited a good part of an hour. Then he came in with some glasses, made an adjustment, set them on the bridge of my nose, took two steps backward. He smiled and said, "Mr. Pinyoun, you look like an executive." I liked him. He had to be a good doctor. He took the glasses off my nose, made another adjustment, set them back on my nose and called his secretary. "Mrs. Bowser, doesn't Mr. Pinyoun look like a million dollars?" I bought two pair of glasses. I wasn't taking a chance of not having those glasses that made me look so good. You know why I bought them! He was enthusiastic about his product and it was rubbing off on me. Hell, he had me glad I was going blind.

Yes, enthusiasm. What does it take to be enthusiastic? First, you have to want to be — that's the whole crux of it. And you must be receptive and want to be enthusiastic.

As Emerson so wisely said, "What is it in life you want? If you want it badly enough, watch out — you'll get it!"

Many years ago, I was on the verge of being drafted into the Army. Now, I didn't know much about the Army except they march, dig holes, and shoot people and none of those appealed to me. So I would have made a lousy soldier. You see, you have to want to.

To have enthusiasm, you must have something to have confidence in.

It's like the dog food company that was having a convention. It was the last hour of the three-day affair and the sales manager was giving them a pep talk, so they'd go out into their respective territories and do a good job. He leaned over the podium and said, "Who has the first dog food company in America?" All the salesmen yelled, "We do!" "Who has the finest advertising department in America?" asked the sales manager. "We do!" yelled the salesmen. "Who has the finest salesmen in America?" he asked. "We do!" was the salesmen's reply. The sales manager hesitated a moment and asked, "Then why the heck aren't we selling more dog food?" A hush fell over the crowded auditorium and finally a man in the back yelled out, "Maybe it's because the dogs don't like the damn stuff." There's your answer. If you don't have confidence in something, you're not going to be enthusiastic.

To be enthusiastic you must have knowledge. There is no substitute for knowledge. I'm reminded of the time the National Cash Register Company was having a convention in Germany. It was at the banquet on the final night that they presented the trophy for the best salesman in all of Germany. When the company president announced the winner a young fellow came forward to receive this most treasured award. As he stood in front of this huge gathering he was excited — almost uncontrolled emotion showed as he tried to keep the tears back. After all, to be the best salesman in all of Germany is a great honor. Finally, the president said, "I'm sure you want to say a few words." The young fellow shifted from one leg to the other and then finally blurted out, "I'll bet there isn't any one in all of Germany that can ask me a question about the National Cash Register that I can't answer." Then he sat down. Now that wasn't much of an acceptance speech, but it certainly summed things up. You must have knowledge.

Also, you must set goals for yourself. You must have short-term goals, and long-term goals and the confidence that you can reach these goals.

I don't like to lose in anything I do; this should be the American way — as long as you play the game fairly, squarely, and decently. I don't like to hear people say, "It's only a game," or "There'll be another day." This attitude can be carried over into one's work, resulting in fear of competition. Too many people today shun success if it asks for hard work or sacrifice.

We are in a fast moving world and many times the man who says "It can't be done" is generally interrupted by someone doing it.

Young people today are in an enviable position, for youth is not considered a handicap as it was years ago. If a young person has intelligence and skill, the road to the top can be his, providing he is ambitious and, above all, has confidence.

The story is told about the young boy in the fifth grade at a mountain school in the hills of West Virginia. It seems that one day the "revenuers" called this boy out of class and told him that they would give him $10 if he would tell them where his paw had his still. The young boy looked the "revenuers" right in the eye and said, "Do you mean that all I got to do is tell you where my Paw's still is and you'll give me $10?" "That's right, son," replied the "Revenuers." "Okay, give me the $10!" replied the young boy. "Oh no, we'll give you the $10 when we come back." The little boy shook his head and said, "I gotta have that $10 now, 'cause you ain't comin' back!"

The confidence and faith that children have is something we tend to forget as we grow older. We get shackled with fears, we become timid and regiment ourselves to a boring routine instead of seeking a better tomorrow.

Life wasn't meant to be easy; it was meant to be challenging. Our American heritage is to constantly strive for a better way, an easier way and more rewarding way. It's this freedom which we are blessed with that we should use.

You say, "What can I do?" Get enthusiastic about you. Get involved in something. Start to learn something and, above all, start the wheels moving. Turn on the steam; build up a head of pressure and don't ever think of quitting. For if you quit today you're closing the door on a better tomorrow.

I want you to be as enthusiastic as this father was. He had just tucked his little daughter in bed and was about to turn off the light. His daughter said, "Daddy, can I have a baby brother?" The father thought for a moment and said, "Why don't you pray and ask God to send you a baby brother?" A few weeks later, the father turned to his daughter and said, "Take my hand. I have a surprise for you upstairs." Upstairs, in the bedroom, was the mother with a tiny baby boy. The little girl was excited.

The father said enthusiastically, "Wait a minute. Look on the other side of the bed." There was another baby boy. The father smiled and said, "Aren't you glad you prayed like Daddy asked you to?" The little girl looked up and said, "Gosh, Daddy, aren't you glad I quit praying when I did?"

TWO BUCKS

Many years ago a shoe company sent two salesmen to Africa to see if they could develop a shoe market. After one week the first salesman wired the home office and said, "I'm coming home; you can't sell shoes here — everyone goes barefooted."

One week later, the other salesman wired the home office and said, "I'll be here indefinitely; I'll sell thousands of pairs of shoes because everyone here is barefooted."

The interesting thing is that both salesmen saw the same thing. One salesman saw it with a negative, defeatest attitude. The other saw it with a positive, successful attitude.

How do you see life? Do you see it through rose-colored glasses, or does it seem dull, drab, and uninteresting?

I still say and will always say that one of the greatest secrets in life is to battle on, not giving up. In spite of hurt, hardships, and set-backs, keep on going. To me, there is no greater lesson. All of this and much more can be yours with a burning desire.

I may stumble, I may tire, I may fall, but God willing I'll fall forward.

George B. Shaw, one of America's greatest thinkers was asked what he would do if he could live his life over again. "I would like to be the man George B. Shaw could have been, but wasn't." Nothing is worth while unless it makes the man.

Life's greatest blessings are the thrill of a new adventure, a new opportunity, a chance of starting all over again. If you have the feeling that this can't happen to you, change your attitude. Opportunities can come your way and every day can be a new challenge.

The trouble with people today is they are shackled by memories of yesterday and fears of tomorrow. In reality our days are what we make them. The road of your success is paved with the material of your thoughts.

Too many people today fail to evaluate their potential, their worth, and their abilities. You can't find your riches until you look within.

There is a story that reminds me of the value some people put on themselves. There was a city fella who got his new Cadillac stuck in the mud on a country road. The fella went over to Zeke, who was a-rockin' on his front porch, and asked him to pull him out of the mudhole. It was a hot day, temperature around 95, and the humidity was high. Well, Zeke gets one mule and pulled for awhile, but that there car was in deep. So Zeke goes and gets another mule and after pulling and pushing for a couple of hours, finally gets the car out of the mudhole. The man asked Zeke what he owed him and Zeke said, "Reckon two dollars would do." When Zeke gets back to the house his wife said, "What'd ya charge that city dude?" "Two bucks," said Zeke. "Two bucks!" yelled his wife, "Ya know, Zeke, sometimes I wish you'd do the pulling and let that mule handle the business end of things."

WHY THIS STORY?

People today are very much like the fellow who did all the planning for the following caper. They have an abundance of ability, but they throw it away. All they needed was direction.

I'm sure you'll enjoy this; perhaps it will strike a nerve. No, I'm not talking about you; but then, you be the judge.

PLAINFIELD STATE TEACHERS

The story you are about to read is absolutely true. The names have been changed to protect those to whom it brought embarrassment.

It happened in New York City where Beaver Jackson lived. He was like any other sports-loving American, except that he had an obsession to coach a football team. He finally decided he would coach Plainfield State Teachers College in the newly formed "middle Eastern League." There were eight teams in this league: Kessler teachers, Hamilton Tech, Williamson teachers, Meares Normal, Eby Institute, Gaines Tech and Butler College.

The first game was all Plainfield State teachers, as they routed Kessler teachers 36-0. That night, coach Beaver Jackson called the New York Chronicle and said, "I'd like to report the results of a football game," and he did so. In Sunday morning's paper, sure enough, there were the results: Plainfield State Teachers 36, Kessler 0. Coach Jackson was jubilant; now he must prepare himself for his Saturday's game with Hamilton Tech whose team consisted of underprivileged northern blacks. The wealthy founder of this school personally financed the football team.

However, on Saturday Plainfield State teachers trounced Hamilton Tech 54-0, holding Hamilton's touted All-American, Charlie Harris, to a minus 32 yards.

Saturday night Coach Jackson called the New York Chronicle Sports Department, and this time he said:

"Who am I talking with?"

"This is sports reporter Bill Calley," was the reply.

"Bill, this is Coach Jackson of the Plainfield State

Teachers. We won our second game today, beating Hamilton Tech 54-0."

"That's great; keep up the good work," was Bill Calley's reply.

(Again, may I emphasize — this actually happened.)

Coach Jackson was up early Sunday morning to read about his victory and, sure enough, it was there — Plainfield State Teachers 54, Hamilton 0.

Coach Jackson was so over-joyed with the showing his team was making that he decided he would start grooming someone for All-American. So he dug down in his bag of tricks and came up with a Chinese fullback named Charles Hubert.

When Saturday rolled around, Coach Jackson was ready for the Williamson Wildcats, who said their flashy quarterback Sammy "Click 'em" Flint would pass them crazy. However, Plainfield's Chinese fullback, Charles Hubert, ran for 385 yards and scored five touchdowns; final score Plainfield State Teachers 63, Williamson Teachers 0.

Coach Jackson called Bill Calley as soon as he got home. "Bill," he said, "this is Coach Jackson. We beat Williamson Teachers 63-0. I might add that my Chinese fullback, Charles Hubert scored five touchdowns and ran for 385 yards." "That's great, Coach," said Bill Calley.

Sunday morning, Coach Jackson met the paper boy; he was so excited about his team winning their first three games and holding the opponents to 0! Sure enough, there it was: Plainfield State Teachers 63, Williamson 0. "Wow," yelled Coach Jackson. "There's a write-up too." It said: "Coach Beaver Jackson's Plainfield State Teachers College won their third straight game, beating Williamson 63-0. The highlight of the game was Charles Hubert, Plainfield's Chinese fullback, who scored 5 touchdowns and ran for 385 yards."

All week, Coach Jackson planned Saturday's game. He decided he must keep his fullback's name in the paper so he'd get recognition, perhaps All-American honors.

Meares Normal school was Plainfield State Teachers' next

opponent. Charles Hubert was at his best as he scored five touchdowns and ran for 402 yards.

There was a casualty in this game. Roche, pronounced "Roshay," Meares' quarterback, dislocated his hip when he completely missed the ball on the kick-off. Coach "Patches" Meares, grandson of the founder of the school, said that Roche would be replaced by Sam Marshall, president of the Alpha Charlie Charlie Fraternity.

When Coach Jackson called Bill Calley to report the game's final score, Plainfield State Teachers 45, Meares Normal 0, he was excited. He had learned that his team had the best record of any college team in the country. Bill Calley was in a receptive mood and wanted more information about this fabulous Plainfield State Teachers team. Coach Jackson was glad to oblige. In fact, he added a bit of imagination when he told Bill Calley this his Chinese fullback always ate rice at half-time, said it gave him more power.

Next week it was more of the same as Eby's Institute was demoralized 54-0.

When Coach Jackson called Bill Calley, Bill did all the talking. "Coach Jackson, I've been waiting for your call. Everyone here is as excited as you are about Plainfield State Teacher's success. In fact, we want to come and interview you and your Chinese fullback and take some pictures. This is going to be one of the greatest sports success stories of the year. When can we come?"

Click! — that was the end of Coach Jackson's coaching career — for Plainfield State teachers existed only in the mind of Coach Jackson.

COUNT YOUR BLESSINGS

If I don't get the things in life
As I pass by this way;
If I don't find the happiness
I should in every day;

If I sometimes feel neglected
In my work and in my play;
And if I keep a-wishin'
For a new and better day;

I stop and count my blessings
As I travel along the road,
Although I may be burdened
With a mighty heavy load—

If I don't get every thing in life
I try not to forget
Of all the things I never want
And I'm never going to get.

Be grateful for what you have
and what you don't have.

—Roy Pinyoun

INDEX

Abilities — 26, 29, 34
Accomplishment — 3, 5, 37, 53, 54, 55, 56, 73, 124, 125, 128
Achievement — 26, 38, 39
Advice — 12
Aim — 17
Ambition — 10, 17, 47, 55, 64, 90, 123
Attitude — 1, 12, 18, 118, 124, 133, 135

Belief — 3, 4, 39, 49, 66, 116, 122
Brain — 17, 115

Challenge — 12
Confidence — 43, 60, 66, 76, 81, 131, 132
Courage — 6, 13, 27, 32, 33, 42, 43, 46, 47, 89, 95, 103, 112
Create — 26

Decision — 45, 54, 58, 67, 81, 113
Dedication — 119
Desire — 8, 23, 37, 56, 57, 88, 91, 122
Determination — 3, 10, 55, 58, 73, 95, 113, 122
Dream — 6, 10, 12, 30, 32, 37, 38, 39, 41, 53, 56, 57, 64, 65, 99, 106, 125
Drive — 17

Education — 8, 14, 33
Effort — 7, 29, 30, 74, 84, 94, 108
Encourage — 37
Energy — 5, 8, 14, 32, 33, 82
Enthusiasm — 6, 7, 28, 56, 67, 81, 130, 131, 132, 139
Environment — 14
Experience — 41

Faith — 9, 18, 44, 57, 67, 69, 81, 94, 95, 122, 133, 135
Fame — 41, 54, 56
Fate — 20, 46
Fortune — 16

Goal — 15, 16, 22, 26, 32, 37, 38, 39, 55, 56, 63, 64, 65, 66, 68, 73, 74, 78, 80, 119, 128, 132
God — 9, 16, 18, 20, 47, 49, 70, 82, 86, 88, 94, 95, 111

Habits — 11, 26
Happiness — 5, 10, 22, 24, 31, 53, 62, 91, 114
Hope — 37

Ideas — 1, 30, 47, 65, 128
Imagination — 14, 17, 80, 122
Intelligence — 5, 10, 56, 92, 133

Knowledge — 5, 18, 31, 41, 53, 73, 77, 80, 116, 117, 126, 132

Life — 3, 5, 11, 12, 20, 21, 22, 25, 30, 33, 44, 45, 53, 54, 56, 61, 64, 65, 67, 70, 75, 76, 85, 90, 91, 104, 106, 133, 135
Live — 4, 69
Love — 14, 15

Mental Attitude — 3, 25
Mind — 3, 15, 25, 26, 37, 39, 64, 70, 94
Money — 24

Opportunity — 1, 8, 9, 13, 15, 25, 58, 64, 68, 69, 84, 96, 99, 120, 124

Perfection — 24
Perseverance — 8, 16

Persistence — 9, 35, 56, 77, 80
Plan — 12
Positive Mental Attitude — 27, 116
Prayer — 18, 19, 20, 83, 94
Progress — 30, 31

Religion — 10
Resourceful — 1, 2
Right — 44

Satisfaction — 33
Sincere — 60
Strong — 13
Success — 3, 5, 10, 11, 12, 18, 19, 23, 25, 26, 28, 29, 32, 33, 35, 44, 49, 54, 55, 56, 57, 58, 65, 76, 77, 78, 80, 89, 90, 91, 102, 112, 116, 128, 135, 136

Talent — 3, 49
Time — 7, 69, 70, 116
Think — 3, 17, 25, 26, 50, 56, 57, 58, 71, 91, 98, 115, 116
Train — 18

Wealth — 8, 14, 41, 54, 66, 69
Win — 5, 29, 38, 44
Wish — 37
Work — 7, 57, 77, 107